2 Speak NOW

COMMUNICATE with CONFIDENCE

Jack C. Richards
David Bohlke

OXFORD
UNIVERSITY PRESS

Welcome to Speak NOW

Communicate *with* Confidence

Communicating with confidence means expressing yourself accurately, fluently, and appropriately. **English in Action** lessons throughout the Student Book present video clips which show students how to use target language in real-life settings. The video is available through Oxford Learn Online Practice, DVD, and on the iTools Classroom Presentation Software CD-ROM.

Online Practice powered by oxfordlearn

Speak Now Online Practice features over 100 engaging self-study activities to help you improve your speaking, pronunciation, and listening skills.

Use the **access card** on the inside back cover to log in at www.oxfordlearn.com/login.

Maximize Speaking

Every activity in every lesson includes a speaking task to ensure students maximize their opportunity to develop confident conversation skills. In each two-page lesson, students learn key **Vocabulary**, practice these new words and develop structured speaking skills through the **Conversation** activity, study new functional language in the **Language Booster** section, and then develop either **Pronunciation** or **Listening** skills in preparation for a communicative **Speak with Confidence** activity.

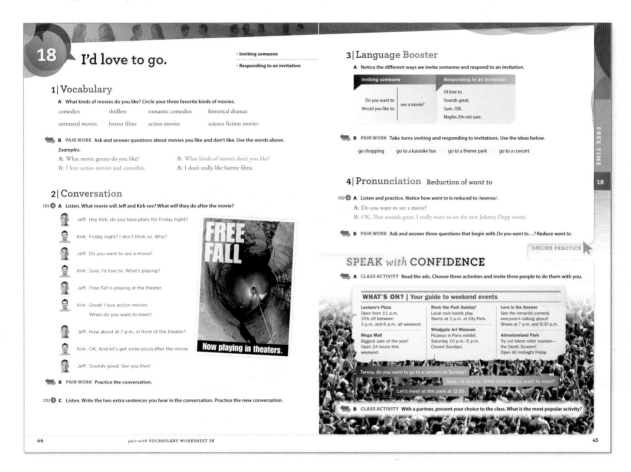

Self-Assessment

Through the **Speak Now** lessons, learners evaluate their progress through role-play situations inspired by the Can-Do statements of the Common European Framework (CEFR).

Scope and Sequence

Scope and Sequence

1 Where are you from?

1 | Vocabulary

A Look at these conversation topics. Check (✓) the people you would talk to about these topics.

Topics	Friends	Family	Anyone	No one
money				
school grades				
personal problems				
hobbies and interests				
home life and family life				
marriage and relationships				

 B **PAIR WORK** Tell your partner which topics are OK and not OK to talk about with specific people.

Example:

A: I think it is OK to talk about hobbies and interests with anyone.

B: I agree. It's not OK to talk about money with friends.

2 | Conversation

CD1 **2** **A** Listen. Where is Nicole from? Who did Brian travel with?

Nicole: Hi. How's it going? I'm Nicole.

Brian: Pretty good. My name's Brian.

Nicole: And where are you from?

Brian: I'm from Canada. And you?

Nicole: Brazil.

Brian: I went to Brazil last year!

Nicole: Really? Wow. Did you travel alone?

Brian: No, I went with friends. It was fun. Listen, I'd better get going.

B **PAIR WORK** Practice the conversation.

CD1 **3** **C** Listen. Write the two extra sentences you hear in the conversation. Practice the new conversation.

pair with VOCABULARY WORKSHEET 1

3 | Language Booster

A Notice the different ways we start and close a conversation.

Starting a conversation		Closing a conversation	
Hi.	My name's…	Listen, I'd better get going.	See you later.
Hello.	How's it going?	Well, I need to go.	Have a nice day.
Excuse me. What's your name?		I've got to run.	Nice talking to you.
Nice day, isn't it?		It's been nice talking to you.	Take care.

 B **PAIR WORK** Take turns starting a conversation. Find out your partner's name and where he or she is from. Then close the conversation.

4 | Pronunciation Contractions

CD1 **4** **A** Listen and practice. Notice how we pronounce contractions.

One syllable			Two syllables		
what's	I'm	she's	isn't	doesn't	wasn't
I've	it's	they've	couldn't	didn't	wouldn't

B **PAIR WORK** Complete the questions to get your partner to answer with *no*. Take turns asking and answering the questions. Pay attention to the pronunciation of contractions.

1. Are you from _____?

2. Do you have any _____?

3. Is your best friend _____?

4. Were you in _____ yesterday?

ONLINE PRACTICE

SPEAK *with* CONFIDENCE

CLASS ACTIVITY Walk around the class and start a conversation with someone. Ask questions about the topics in the Vocabulary section. Then close the conversation. Talk to at least five people.

2 I'm tall and thin.

1 | Vocabulary

A How do you describe people? Write the words in the correct categories.

elderly	pretty
good-looking	short
handsome	tall
heavy	thin
middle-aged	young

height	build	age	looks

B   PAIR WORK Take turns describing yourself. Use the words above.

Example:

A: I'm thin and a little short.

B: I am tall. I also think I look young for my age.

2 | Conversation

CD1 **5** **A** Listen. Who is Nathan looking for? What is she wearing?

Nathan: Excuse me. **I'm looking for my wife.**

Clerk: What does she look like?

Nathan: Well, she's tall and thin.

Clerk: **Does she have red hair?**

Nathan: No. **My wife has dark brown hair.**

Clerk: What's she wearing?

Nathan: A blue skirt and a white blouse.

Clerk: **Is that her by the changing room?**

Nathan: Yes. I guess she wants that coat.

B   PAIR WORK Practice the conversation. Then exchange the blue and green words above with the words below and practice it again.

Nathan: **I can't find my wife.** ⟩ Clerk: **Is her hair red?** ⟩ Nathan: **Her hair is dark brown.** ⟩ Clerk: **Is that her over there?**

3 | Language Booster

A Notice the different ways we ask about and describe people's appearances.

Asking about appearance	Describing appearance
What does he/she look like?	She's pretty.
	He's very good-looking.
How tall is he/she?	He's She's { really tall. / medium height. / a little short. }
Does he/she have red hair?	No, he/she has dark brown hair.

B **PAIR WORK** Take turns asking about and describing the appearances of your family members.

4 | Listening

 CD1 **6** **A** Listen. Two friends are talking about people at a party. Write the correct number of the person in the picture.

1. Paula

2. Reggie

3. Wally

4. Adam

5. Valerie

CD1 **6** **B** Listen again. Rewrite these sentences so they are true. Tell your partner your answers.

1. Paula is in her late thirties. 2. Wally is medium height. 3. Adam is Paula's younger brother.

ONLINE PRACTICE

SPEAK *with* CONFIDENCE

GROUP WORK In groups of four, each person thinks of a famous movie star, singer, or athlete. Then take turns asking ten *yes* or *no* questions to guess each person.

Possible questions
Is…single/married?
Is…American/Japanese/Brazilian?
Is…in his/her teens/twenties/thirties?
Does…sing hip-hop/pop/rock 'n' roll?
Does…play soccer/baseball/tennis?

3 | Alice is more serious.

- **Asking about personalities**
- **Describing personalities**

1 | Vocabulary

A Look at these words that describe personality. Match them with the correct descriptions.

| a. confident | b. creative | c. forgetful | d. funny | e. impatient | f. outgoing |

_____ 1. Penny doesn't like to wait.

_____ 2. Ahmed never remembers our plans.

_____ 3. Maria is always so sure of herself.

_____ 4. Kerry makes people laugh.

_____ 5. Patricia makes friends easily.

_____ 6. Jae-soon is always drawing.

B PAIR WORK Take turns describing people you know who have the personalities above.

2 | Conversation

CD1 7 **A** Listen. How are Mary's children similar? How are they different?

B PAIR WORK Practice the conversation. Then exchange the blue and green words above with the words below and practice it again.

Ling: **Are they very similar?** Mary: Matilda is playful. Ling: **What's her sister like?** Mary: She's shy.

pair with VOCABULARY WORKSHEET 3

3 | Language Booster

A Notice the different ways we ask about and describe personalities.

Asking about personalities	Describing personalities
What are they like?	They're both very creative. Alice is outgoing, but Matilda is shy.
How would you describe him/her? What's he/she like?	I'd say he's/she's outgoing and funny. He's/She's smart, but a little forgetful.
Do you think you're patient?	Yes. I'm a very patient person. Not really. In fact, I can be very impatient.

 B **PAIR WORK** Take turns asking about and describing the personalities of your friends.

4 | Listening

 CD1 **8** **A** Listen to descriptions of three people. Circle the words that describe them.

	What are they like?			What else do you learn?
1. Nora	outgoing	shy	confident	
2. Simon	creative	funny	smart	
3. Caley	hardworking	patient	forgetful	

CD1 **8** **B** Listen again. Write one other thing you learned about each person.

 C **PAIR WORK** Describe someone you know with one of the personalities above.

ONLINE PRACTICE

SPEAK with CONFIDENCE

A Check (✓) the statements that describe you. Then write one true and one false statement about yourself.

☐ I sometimes forget things.   ☐ I don't worry about much.

☐ I'm always on time.   ☐ I'm usually very patient.

_____   _____

B **GROUP WORK** Say one of the statements above. Other students take turns guessing if it's true.

I'm always on time. I'm never late.

That's not true! You came to class late today!

4 All of my friends text.

• Talking about quantities

1 | Vocabulary

A Which word doesn't belong? Cross it out. Then compare with a partner.

1. I send ~~social networks~~ / e-mails / texts.

2. I play *basketball* / *bowling* / *games*.

3. I want to get *engaged* / *married* / *wedding*.

4. I take a *bus* / *drive* / *taxi* to class.

5. I do *swimming* / *yoga* / *aerobics*.

6. I like to go *dancing* / *hiking* / *singing*.

7. I have a *pet* / *busy* / *job*.

8. I keep a *blog* / *homework* / *diary*.

B **PAIR WORK** Take turns guessing what you think is true about your partner. Use the words above.

Example:

A: I think you text a lot.

B: That's right. I do. I think you like to go hiking.

2 | Conversation

CD1 ⑨ **A** Listen. What is Luke doing? What does Luke often do on his phone?

Ellen: What are you doing?

Luke: I'm just sending an e-mail.

Ellen: Do you always use your phone to send e-mails?
All of my friends text these days.

Luke: Some of my friends text, some don't. That e-mail was to my dad.

Ellen: So, what else do you use your phone for?

Luke: I often use it to play games. A lot of my friends
watch movies, but I find the screen too small.

Ellen: Do you use it for social networking?

Luke: Sure, all the time. Say, I don't think we're friends online…

B **PAIR WORK** Practice the conversation.

CD1 ⑩ **C** Listen. Write the two extra sentences you hear in the conversation. Practice the new conversation.

pair with VOCABULARY WORKSHEET 4

3 | Language Booster

A Notice the different ways we talk about quantities.

Talking about quantities

All of		
Most of		
Many of	my friends	text these days.
A lot of	the people I know	bring our laptops to class.
Some of	our classmates	have blogs.
Not many of	us	
A few of		
None of		

 B   PAIR WORK Complete these sentences with your own ideas. Then tell your partner.

All of the people in my family…   Most of the students at this school…

A few of my friends…   None of us in this class…

4 | Pronunciation Reduction of *of*

 A   Listen and practice. Notice how *of* is often pronounced /əv/ before vowel sounds but reduced to /ə/ before consonant sounds.

of + vowel sound	*of* + consonant sound
all of **o**ur classmates	all of **m**y classmates
a lot of **E**nglish speakers	a lot of **K**orean speakers
a few of **u**s in this class	a few of **th**eir friends

 B   PAIR WORK Practice the sentences in the Language Booster section. Pay attention to the pronunciation of *of*.

ONLINE PRACTICE

SPEAK *with* CONFIDENCE

A   CLASS ACTIVITY Choose one of these questions or think of your own. Ask it to as many people in your class as you can. Take notes on all of the answers.

How do you get to class?

Why are you studying English?

What do you like to do on the weekends?

B   GROUP WORK Share your results. Did the results surprise you?

CD1 11

English in Action

1 | Preview

PAIR WORK Look at this picture of Casey. Write the words you think best describe her.

Casey   Tom

1. _____   2. _____   3. _____   4. _____

2 | Practice

A Watch the video. Mark the statements T (true) or F (false).

_____ 1. Eric is texting while he studies.

_____ 2. Jill is waiting for her sister Casey.

_____ 3. Casey is going to stay for a few weeks.

_____ 4. Jill and Casey are similar.

_____ 5. Eric knows Casey from high school.

_____ 6. Casey is taking a taxi.

_____ 7. Casey doesn't like fashion.

_____ 8. Casey is 24 years old.

B Watch the video again. Rewrite the false statements so they are true.

3 | Discuss

GROUP WORK Answer the questions.

1. Do you have friends who are creative? What do they do?

2. Do you use any social networks? Why or why not?

3. Do you have online friends you've never met?

CONFIDENCE BOOSTER   Student A: Turn to page 82.
Student B: Turn to page 90.

FRIENDS & FAMILY

1

2

3

4

VIDEO

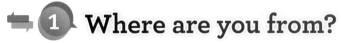

Speak NOW

1 Where are you from?

A Student A: Start a conversation with Student B and ask two questions. Then close the conversation.

Student B: Answer Student A's questions.

B Now change roles.

I can start a conversation.
☐ Very well   ☐ I need more practice.

I can close a conversation.
☐ Very well   ☐ I need more practice.

See Language Booster page 3.

2 I'm tall and thin.

A Student A: Think of someone in your class and describe him or her. Don't say who it is. Student B will guess the person.

Student B: Listen to Student A's description of someone in your class. Ask questions and try to guess the person.

B Now change roles.

I can ask about appearance.
☐ Very well   ☐ I need more practice.

I can describe appearance.
☐ Very well   ☐ I need more practice.

See Language Booster page 5.

3 Alice is more serious.

A Student A: Choose two people both you and Student B know. Describe their personalities.

Student B: Listen to Student A. Ask questions or add ideas of your own.

B Now change roles.

I can ask about personalities.
☐ Very well   ☐ I need more practice.

I can describe personalities.
☐ Very well   ☐ I need more practice.

See Language Booster page 7.

4 All of my friends text.

Student A and Student B: Take turns completing the sentences with your own ideas.

Most of the people I know…

Many of the celebrities today…

None of my family members…

A lot of people I see every day…

I can talk about quantities.
☐ Very well   ☐ I need more practice.

See Language Booster page 9.

I've never had Thai food.

• **Asking about experiences**

• **Describing experiences**

1 | Vocabulary

A Look at these types of cuisines. Circle the ones you have tried.

American	Chinese	Turkish	Italian	Thai	Indian
Vietnamese	Mexican	Korean	Japanese	Moroccan	Brazilian

 B **PAIR WORK** Tell your partner a dish from a cuisine you have tried.

Example:

A: Can you name a Korean dish?

B: Bibimbap is a famous Korean dish.

B: Do you know any Italian dishes?

A: Yes. Risotto is Italian.

2 | Conversation

CD1 12 **A** **Listen. Who has tried Mexican food? Where do Kent and Lori decide to go?**

 B **PAIR WORK** Practice the conversation. Then exchange the blue and green words above with the words below and practice it again.

Lori: **Have you ever had French food?** Kent: **But I feel like Asian tonight.**

Lori: **The soups are to die for!** Kent: **Do you know a nice place?**

3 | Language Booster

A Notice the different ways we ask about and describe experiences.

Asking about experiences	Describing experiences
Have you ever **had** / **tried** Mexican food?	Yes, I have.
	Yes, I've had it several times.
	No, I haven't. I've never tried it.
Have you ever been to a Turkish restaurant?	No, but I've always wanted to go to one.
What Japanese dishes have you tried?	I've had sushi and ramen.

 B PAIR WORK Take turns asking about and describing food experiences.

4 | Listening

CD1 ⑬ **A** Listen. Four people are talking about foods they've tried. Number the foods from 1 to 4 in the order you hear them.

CD1 ⑬ **B** Listen again. How do they describe the taste of the food? Write the words.

1. _____ 2. _____ 3. _____ 4. _____

 C PAIR WORK Take turns telling your partner which foods you haven't tried and if you'd like to try them.

ONLINE PRACTICE

SPEAK with CONFIDENCE

 A CLASS ACTIVITY Complete the questions. Then go around the class and find someone who has done each thing. Write the person's name and find out if he or she liked it.

Have you ever...	Name	Liked it?
eaten _____ (a food)?		yes / no
drunk _____ (a drink)?		yes / no
been to _____ (name of restaurant)?		yes / no

 B PAIR WORK Tell your partner two interesting things you learned about your classmates.

6 First, grill the bread.

1 | Vocabulary

A Look at these ways of preparing food. Add at least one more food to each column.

grill	bake	fry	steam	boil	microwave
meat	cake	fish	vegetables	noodles	frozen dinner

 B **PAIR WORK** Take turns telling your partner the best way to prepare the different foods.

Example:

A: I think the best way to prepare vegetables is to steam them.

2 | Conversation

CD1 **14** **A** Listen. What do you need to make bruschetta? What do you do after you rub the bread with garlic?

Joel: What are you making?

Tara: Bruschetta. Have you ever tried it?

Joel: No. How do you make it?

Tara: First, grill the bread. Make sure you grill both sides. Then rub the bread with garlic.

Joel: OK. It smells good.

Tara: Next, pour olive oil on the bread. Don't pour too much, just a little. After that, put on some chopped tomatoes. Finally, add salt, pepper, and a basil leaf. Try one!

 B **PAIR WORK** Practice the conversation.

CD1 **15** **C** Listen. Write the two extra sentences you hear in the conversation. Practice the new conversation.

3 | Language Booster

A Notice the different ways we give instructions and remind someone of something.

Giving a series of instructions	Reminding someone of something
First, grill the bread. Then rub the bread with garlic. Next, pour olive oil on the bread. After that, put on some chopped tomatoes. Finally, add salt, pepper, and a basil leaf.	Make sure you Remember to grill both sides. Be sure to use fresh tomatoes. Don't forget to

 B **PAIR WORK** Number these steps for boiling an egg in order from 1 to 5. Then take turns giving these instructions. Use sequences words *first, then, next, after that,* and *finally.*

_____ Add water to the pot.   _____ Boil the water.   _____ Cook for 12 minutes.

_____ Put an egg in a pot.   _____ Cool the egg with cold water.

C **PAIR WORK** Give the instructions again. This time add these reminders in the correct place.

Don't forget to set a timer.   Make sure the water covers the egg.

4 | Pronunciation Consonant clusters

CD1 16 **A** Listen and practice. Notice how the two consonant sounds at the beginning of a word are pronounced together. Each of these words is one syllable.

1. **sm**ell   2. **sk**ip   3. **sp**ice   4. **st**eam   5. **sn**ack   6. **fr**y   7. **gl**ad

 B **PAIR WORK** Practice these sentences. Pay attention to how you pronounce consonant clusters.

1. **Pl**ease **sl**ice some **br**ead.   2. Never **sk**ip **br**eakfast.   3. Put a **sn**ack on a **pl**ate.

ONLINE PRACTICE

SPEAK *with* CONFIDENCE

A Look at the picture. Choose a snack you can make with at least three items. You can add your own items. Write the steps to make your snack.

B **GROUP WORK** Take turns explaining how to make your snack.

I can make an egg salad.

How do you make it?

First, you boil the eggs.

7 The service is great.

1 | Vocabulary

A Do you eat at these places very often? Rank them from 1 (most often) to 8 (least often).

_____ café   _____ snack bar   _____ buffet restaurant   _____ fast-food restaurant

_____ food cart   _____ cafeteria   _____ food court   _____ fine dining restaurant

B **PAIR WORK** Tell your partner which places you go to most often and least often.

Example:

A: I eat at food courts most often.

B: Really? I eat at cafés most often. Where do you eat least often?

2 | Conversation

CD1 **17** **A** Listen. What does _The Pink Peppercorn_ serve? What doesn't Sarah like about the restaurant?

 Kit: So what are you in the mood for?

 Sarah: Have you tried that new restaurant near the subway station?

 Kit: **You mean _The Pink Peppercorn?_**

 Sarah: Yeah. That's the one.

 Kit: No, I haven't yet. What's it like?

 Sarah: It's pretty good. They serve a lot of curries and noodles dishes. **And their prices are reasonable.** Most of the dishes cost about $10.

 Kit: **That's pretty good.** What's the service like?

 Sarah: **The service is really slow, but otherwise it's a nice place.**

 Kit: I think I'll try it!

 B **PAIR WORK** Practice the conversation. Then exchange the blue and green words above with the words below and practice it again.

Kit: **Are you talking about _The Pink Peppercorn?_**	Sarah: **And their prices aren't bad.**
Kit: **That sounds great!**	Sarah: **The service isn't so great, but it's worth a try.**

3 | Language Booster

A Notice the different ways we describe restaurants.

> **Describing restaurants**
>
> The food is fantastic/pretty good/so-so.
> They serve a lot of curries and noodle dishes.
> The prices are expensive/reasonable/fairly cheap.
> It attracts a lot of office workers at lunch.
> The service is really great/slow.
> It has a fun/relaxed atmosphere.

 B **PAIR WORK** Take turns describing your favorite restaurant. Use the words below.

food   prices   location   service   atmosphere

4 | Listening

CD1 **18** **A** Listen. Two people are discussing a restaurant. Number the things from 1 to 5 in the order you hear them.

_____ a. service   _____ b. atmosphere   _____ c. location   _____ d. prices   _____ e. food

CD1 **18** **B** Listen again. Mark + (positive) or − (negative) for the opinion you hear about each thing.

_____ a. service   _____ b. atmosphere   _____ c. location   _____ d. prices   _____ e. food

 C **PAIR WORK** Tell your partner what you think is important when choosing a restaurant.

ONLINE PRACTICE

SPEAK *with* CONFIDENCE

 A **PAIR WORK** Imagine you and your partner are owners of a restaurant. Answer the questions below.

What is the name of your restaurant?

What kind of food does your restaurant serve? What are the prices?

Where is your restaurant located?

What kind of atmosphere and decoration does it have? How is it special?

 B **GROUP WORK** Present your restaurant. Choose one restaurant from your group.

C **CLASS ACTIVITY** Present the restaurant. Vote on one restaurant the class would like to go to.

Are you ready to order?

- Taking orders
- Ordering food

1 | Vocabulary

A Look at these items on a restaurant menu. Add them to the correct category.

vegetable lasagna	spinach dip
vanilla ice cream	fried chicken
mashed potatoes	apple pie
shrimp cocktail	French fries
steak	spring rolls
chocolate cake	steamed rice

appetizers	main dishes	side dishes	desserts

 B PAIR WORK Take turns telling your partner which foods you think fits in each category.

2 | Conversation

CD1 **19** **A Listen. Which side dish does the customer order? Does she order an appetizer?**

Welcome to Zippy's. Are you ready to order?

Yes, I'd like the fried chicken, please.

1

Would you like mashed potatoes, French fries, or steamed rice with that?

Hm... I'll take steamed rice.

2

Anything to drink?

I'll have the peach iced tea.

3

Anything else? Would you like to start with an appetizer?

No, I'm saving room for dessert.

4

 B PAIR WORK Practice the conversation.

CD1 **20** **C Listen. Write the two extra sentences you hear in the conversation. Practice the new conversation.**

pair with VOCABULARY WORKSHEET 8

3 | Language Booster

A Notice how we take orders and order food in a restaurant.

Taking orders	Ordering food
Are you ready to order?	Yes, thank you.
May I take your order?	Not yet. Can I have another minute?
What would you like?	I'd like / I'll have the fried chicken, please.
Would you like an appetizer? dessert? something to drink?	No, thanks. / Maybe later. / Yes. I'll have the peach iced tea.

 B **PAIR WORK** Imagine you are in a restaurant. Take turns ordering food and taking the order. Use the words in the Vocabulary section.

Example:

A: May I take your order?

B: Yes, I'd like the vegetable lasagna, please.

4 Pronunciation Intonation choice questions

 A Listen and practice. Notice the intonation rises and then falls in questions that ask a choice.

1. Hot tea or iced tea?   2. Would you like mashed potatoes, French fries, or steamed rice?

 B **PAIR WORK** Complete the questions below with your own ideas. Then practice them. Pay attention to your intonation.

1. Apple pie or _____?   2. Do you want to go to a café, _____, or _____?

ONLINE PRACTICE

SPEAK *with* CONFIDENCE

PAIR WORK Look at the menu below. Take turns taking an order and ordering food.

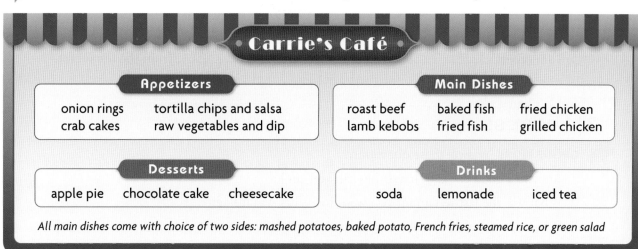

Carrie's Café

Appetizers

onion rings   tortilla chips and salsa
crab cakes   raw vegetables and dip

Main Dishes

roast beef   baked fish   fried chicken
lamb kebobs   fried fish   grilled chicken

Desserts

apple pie   chocolate cake   cheesecake

Drinks

soda   lemonade   iced tea

All main dishes come with choice of two sides: mashed potatoes, baked potato, French fries, steamed rice, or green salad

English in Action

1 | Preview

 **PAIR WORK** Tom is cooking. Write the ingredients you see.

1. _____   3. _____   5. _____

2. _____   4. _____   6. _____

2 | Practice

A Watch the video. Eric and Tom are talking about dishes. Check (✓) the foods Tom has tried before.

_____ 1. Indian   _____ 2. Japanese   _____ 3. pasta

B Watch the video again. Complete these sentences.

1. Eric tries to teach Tom how to cook _____.

2. After you fry the vegetables in a pan, you need to add _____.

3. Eric leaves Tom alone because _____.

4. Tom burns _____.

5. Tom orders _____ from the restaurant.

3 | Discuss

 GROUP WORK Answer these questions.

1. Are you a good cook? What dishes can you cook?

2. What was the last restaurant you went to? What was it like?

3. What restaurant do you eat at the most? What do you usually order?

CONFIDENCE BOOSTER   Student A: Turn to page 83.
Student B: Turn to page 91.

RESTAURANTS

5

6

7

8

VIDEO

5 ▸ I've never had Thai food.

A Student A: Find out a food (or a type of food) that Student B has tried. Ask follow-up questions.

Student B: Answer Student A's questions.

B Now change roles.

I can ask about experiences.
☐ Very well   ☐ I need more practice.

I can describe experiences.
☐ Very well   ☐ I need more practice.

See Language Booster page 13.

6 ▸ First, grill the bread.

A Student A: Tell Student B how to make a dish or snack. Remind him or her of things to remember while preparing the dish.

Student B: Listen to Student A describe a recipe. Ask follow-up questions.

B Now change roles.

I can give a series of instructions.
☐ Very well   ☐ I need more practice.

I can remind someone of something.
☐ Very well   ☐ I need more practice.

See Language Booster page 15.

7 ▸ The service is great.

A Student A: Tell Student B about a restaurant you like. Describe its food, prices, atmosphere, and service. Say what you like and don't like about it.

Student B: Listen to Student A describe a restaurant. Ask follow-up questions.

B Now change roles.

I can describe a restaurant.
☐ Very well   ☐ I need more practice.

See Language Booster page 17.

8 ▸ Are you ready to order?

A Student A: You are a customer in your favorite restaurant. Student B is the server. Order whatever you want.

Student B: You are a server in a restaurant. Student A is a customer. Take his or her order.

B Now change roles.

I can take an order.
☐ Very well   ☐ I need more practice.

I can order food.
☐ Very well   ☐ I need more practice.

See Language Booster page 19.

ONLINE PRACTICE

9 I have a sore throat.

• **Describing health problems**

• **Making suggestions**

1 | Vocabulary

A Look at the words below. Circle the health problems you've had.

a cold	a headache	a sore throat
a fever	a sore back	a stomachache
a cough	the flu	dry skin

 B **PAIR WORK** Tell your partner what you usually do when you have one of the problems above. Use the ideas below or your own ideas.

get rest	see a doctor	stay in bed	take some medicine	ignore the problem

2 | Conversation

CD1 22 **A** Listen. What is Leila's problem? What does Tracey suggest?

> Hi, Tracey. I'm not feeling too well.
>
> Oh? **What's the matter, Leila?**
>
> **1** No. I'm fine, really. I think I just have a cold.

> I have a sore throat.
>
> That's too bad. I hope it's not the flu. Have you seen a doctor?
>
> **2** Good idea. **Can you take notes for me in class?**

> **3** You have a fever. **Why don't you go home and rest?**

> Sure. I hope you feel better soon.
>
> Thanks.
>
> **4**

 B **PAIR WORK** Practice the conversation. Then exchange the blue and green words above with the words below and practice it again.

Mary: **What's wrong?**	Leila: **I have a headache.**

Mary: **Why don't you take some aspirin?**	Leila: **Can I call you later?**

3 | Language Booster

A Notice the different ways we describe health problems and make suggestions.

Describing health problems	Making suggestions
I have a cold/the flu.	Why don't you go home and rest?
I have a sore throat/back.	It's a good idea to drink hot tea.
My stomach/knee hurts.	Try not to eat late at night.
I can't sleep at night.	I suggest seeing a doctor.

 B **PAIR WORK** Take turns describing the health problems below and making suggestions.

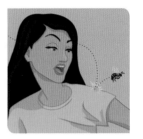

a stiff neck   insomnia   a sprained ankle   a bee sting

4 | Listening

CD1 **23** **A** Listen to four conversations. Circle the problem that best matches each conversation.

1. a sprained hand / a broken hand

2. a sore throat / a stomachache

3. an eye problem / an ear problem

4. dry skin / a headache

CD1 **23** **B** Listen again. Mark the statements T (true) or F (false).

1. _____ The accident happened last week.
   _____ He went to the doctor.

2. _____ She took some medicine for it.
   _____ They both have the same problem.

3. _____ They are very sore.
   _____ She has been to see a doctor.

4. _____ She is feeling better.
   _____ He suggests taking a cold bath.

ONLINE PRACTICE

SPEAK with CONFIDENCE

A **CLASS ACTIVITY** Divide the class in half. One half chooses and describes health problems. The other half gives suggestions. Describe your health problem or make suggestions to four students.

B **CLASS ACTIVITY** Now change roles.

10 What should I do?

1 | Vocabulary

A Look at some things you can do at home to keep healthy and fit. Check (✓) the things you do to keep fit.

_____ climb stairs   _____ dance to music   _____ walk around the neighborhood

_____ ride a bike   _____ jump up and down   _____ follow a workout video

_____ do chores   _____ play an active video game   _____ rearrange the furniture

 B **PAIR WORK** Tell your partner what you do to keep healthy and fit.

Example:

A: I climb the stairs to keep healthy.

B: That's a great idea. I dance to music.

A: Me too! It's fun and a great way to exercise.

2 | Conversation

CD1 24 **A** Listen. What does Luisa think Alex should do? What does she think he shouldn't do?

Alex: I've been so tired lately. I never seem to have enough energy. Should I join a gym?

Luisa: Gyms can be expensive. There are simple ways to exercise at home.

Alex: Like what?

Luisa: If I were you, I'd climb the stairs or dance to music. You should do something active that you enjoy. Are you getting enough sleep?

Alex: Sure. I sleep about ten hours a day.

Luisa: That's too much. Getting too much sleep can make you feel tired. You should try to sleep eight hours a day.

 B **PAIR WORK** Practice the conversation.

CD1 25 **C** Listen. Write the two extra sentences you hear in the conversation. Practice the new conversation.

3 | Language Booster

A Notice the different ways we ask for and give advice.

Asking for advice	Giving advice
What should I do?	I think you should exercise more.
What do you think I should do?	If I were you, I'd climb stairs.
	I don't think you should join a gym.
Should I join a gym?	You shouldn't join a gym.

 B PAIR WORK Take turns choosing a situation below and giving advice.

You want a healthier diet.   You have difficulty waking up.

4 | Pronunciation Syllables

CD1 **26** **A** Listen and practice. Notice the number of syllables in these words.

One syllable	Two syllables	Three syllables	Four syllables
chores	music	furniture	conversation
stairs	fitness	video	exercises

CD1 **27** **B** Listen. How many syllables do you hear? Write the number.

_____ a. healthier   _____ c. shouldn't   _____ e. considering   _____ g. marathon

_____ b. chores   _____ d. difficulty   _____ f. sleep   _____ h. active

 C PAIR WORK Practice the words in part B. Take turns making sentences with the words.

ONLINE PRACTICE

SPEAK *with* CONFIDENCE

 A PAIR WORK Imagine you want to do the things below. Take turns asking for and giving advice.

cut caffeine from your diet	have less stress in your life
get enough sleep	eat less sugar
watch less TV	spend less money

 B GROUP WORK Join another pair and compare your advice. Who has the best advice for each situation?

11 I'd love to try that!

1 | Vocabulary

A Look at these fitness activities and the calories they burn in one hour. Which activities burn the most calories?

activity	calories burned	activity	calories burned
ballroom dancing	325–500	running	985–1,075
bowling	175–280	skiing	510–765
ice skating	450–760	swimming	510–765
walking	305–470	tae kwon do	730–1,090
racquetball	510–765	tai chi	215–330

B **PAIR WORK** Tell your partner which fitness activities you like to do. Give reasons for your response.

Example:

A: I like to play racquetball. It helps me relieve stress.

B: I like to ski. I like outdoor activities and I love the snow.

2 | Conversation

CD1 28 **A** Listen. Why is Peter interested in ballroom dancing? Why is Rachel interested in tai chi?

Rachel: **I really need to get more exercise.**

Peter: Me too. We could take classes at the sports center.

There's racquetball, boxing, swimming—

Rachel: Oh, I wouldn't really like those. They seem like a lot of hard work.

Peter: Well, how about a class in ballroom dancing? **I'd love to try that!**

Rachel: **Really?** Why is that?

Peter: **Because I'd learn something new.** And I can do it with someone else.

Rachel: I think it would be boring. I'd like to try something more relaxing, like tai chi.

B **PAIR WORK** Practice the conversation. Then exchange the blue and green words above with the words below and practice it again.

Rachel: **I want to be more fit.** ⋙ Peter: **I've always wanted to try it.**

Rachel: **Are you serious?** ⋙ Peter: **I imagine it's a fun workout.**

3 | Language Booster

A Notice the different ways we express wants and intentions, and give reasons.

Expressing wants and intentions	Giving reasons
I really want to / I'd like to / I've always wanted to — take a dancing class.	I need to get some exercise.
	I'd learn something new.
I don't want to / I wouldn't like to / I'd never — learn tae kwon do.	It seems like a lot of hard work.
	I think it would be boring.

B **PAIR WORK** Take turns expressing wants and intentions, and giving reasons. Use the activities from the Vocabulary section.

4 | Listening

 A Listen. People are describing fitness activities. Number them from 1 to 4 in the order you hear them.

archery

kayaking

table tennis

water aerobics

 B Listen again. Why do they want to try the activities? Write one reason.

1. _____

2. _____

3. _____

4. _____

ONLINE PRACTICE

SPEAK *with* CONFIDENCE

GROUP WORK Read about the fitness activities below. Tell three classmates what you would and wouldn't like to try. Give reasons for your response.

Interesting Fitness Activities

Zumba is a Latin-inspired dance. It is a popular and fun exercise. You can do aerobics and dance at the same time.

Forza means *strength* in Italian. You use a wooden sword to practice Japanese sword-fighting techniques.

Bosu is also known as *blue half-ball*. You can stand on it, lie on it, place your knees on it, or push your arms off it.

12 Soccer is more exciting!

• Asking for comparisons
....
• Making comparisons

1 | Vocabulary

A Write the names of sports in the correct category.

baseball	boxing	hockey
basketball	cycling	tennis
bowling	fishing	volleyball

indoor sports	outdoor sports

 B **PAIR WORK** Tell your partner which sports you think belong to each category.

Example:

A: I think basketball belongs in outdoor sports.

B: I don't. I think it belongs in indoor sports.

2 | Conversation

CD1 ⓖ **A** Listen. What does Doug think of tennis? Who prefers golf to tennis?

 Celine: So, I just got this great new sports channel. All sports, all the time.

 Doug: Cool. So, what should we watch?

 Celine: Let's see...how about tennis?

 Doug: Um, is it OK if we watch something different? Tennis is kind of boring to watch.

 Celine: Sure. Golf is more interesting than tennis, don't you think?

 Doug: Not really. I think golf is less interesting than tennis. I do like soccer. It's my favorite.

 Celine: Mine too, but there are no soccer games today. Say, do you want to go for a walk?

 B **PAIR WORK** Practice the conversation.

CD1 ㉛ **C** Listen. Write the two extra sentences you hear in the conversation. Practice the new conversation.

pair with **VOCABULARY WORKSHEET 12**

3 | Language Booster

A Notice the different ways we ask for and make comparisons.

Asking for comparisons		Making comparisons
Which is more interesting	to watch?	Golf is not as interesting to watch as tennis.
Which is easier	to play?	Volleyball is easier to play than hockey.
Which is more difficult	to learn?	Boxing is much more difficult to learn than bowling.
Which do you like more?		I like soccer more than tennis.

 B **PAIR WORK** Take turns asking for and making comparisons. Use the words in the Vocabulary section.

Example:

A: Which is easier to learn: tennis or hockey?

B: Tennis is easier to learn than hockey.

4 | Pronunciation Silent syllables

CD1 **32** **A** Listen and practice. Notice how some words can have silent syllables.

1. favorite   3. frightening   5. interesting   7. different

2. generally   4. average   6. comfortable

 B **PAIR WORK** Practice these sentences. Pay attention to the silent syllables.

1. Tennis is my favorite sport.
2. Baseball and football are very different.

3. Volleyball is an interesting sport.
4. I'm not comfortable watching boxing.

ONLINE PRACTICE

SPEAK *with* CONFIDENCE

 A **GROUP WORK** Discuss the questions below and make comparisons. Ask follow-up questions.

Which is more frightening: bungee jumping or parachuting?

Do you think baseball is as exciting as soccer?

Which is more dangerous: rock climbing or scuba diving?

Do you think American football is as easy to play as soccer?

B **GROUP WORK** Replace the activities in part A with your own ideas. Ask the questions again.

English in Action

1 | Preview

 PAIR WORK Eric is not very fit. What advice do you think his doctor gave him? Check (✓) your guesses. Then compare with a partner.

_____ 1. eat more vegetables

_____ 2. drink less coffee

_____ 3. take vitamins

_____ 4. exercise every day

_____ 5. play a sport

_____ 6. see a doctor regularly

_____ 7. do not eat any meat

_____ 8. drink more juice

2 | Practice

A Watch the video. What advice did the doctor give Eric? Did you guess correctly?

B Watch the video again. Circle the correct answers to the questions.

1. When was Eric's doctor's appointment?
   a. last month   b. yesterday   c. last week

2. What does the doctor want Eric to do?
   a. change his diet   b. go on a diet   c. eat more meals

3. What does the doctor say is a good idea to stay fit?
   a. eat fewer vegetables   b. give up meat   c. stop drinking coffee

4. How often does Eric bowl?
   a. four times a week   b. every day   c. on the weekends

5. Where does Eric play tennis?
   a. at the park   b. at home   c. at the gym

3 | Discuss

GROUP WORK Answer the questions.

1. What advice would you give someone who wanted to be more fit?

2. Do you have a healthy diet? Is there anything you should eat more of or less of?

3. What do you think of active video games? Have you ever played them? Do you consider them exercise?

Ⓒ**ONFIDENCE BOOSTER** Student A: Turn to page 84. Student B: Turn to page 92.

HEALTH

9

10

11

12

VIDEO

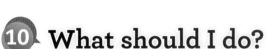

Speak NOW

9 **I have a sore throat.**

A Student A: Imagine you have a health problem.
Tell Student B about it.

Student B: Give two suggestions to Student A.

B Now change roles.

I can describe a health problem.
☐ Very well   ☐ I need more practice.

I can make a suggestion.
☐ Very well   ☐ I need more practice.

See Language Booster page 23.

10 **What should I do?**

A Student A: Choose two of these situations. Ask Student B for advice.

You want a healthier lifestyle.	You want to have less stress.
You want to lose weight.	You want to find a new hobby.

Student B: Listen and give Student A advice. Include at least two
things he or she should or shouldn't do.

B Now change roles.

I can ask for advice.
☐ Very well   ☐ I need more practice.

I can give advice.
☐ Very well   ☐ I need more practice.

See Language Booster page 25.

11 **I'd love to try that!**

A Student A: Tell Student B about a fitness activity you would like
to try, and why.

Student B: Tell Student A if you would like to try the activity he or
she mentions, and why or why not.

B Now change roles.

I can express wants and intentions.
☐ Very well   ☐ I need more practice.

I can give reasons.
☐ Very well   ☐ I need more practice.

See Language Booster page 27.

12 **Soccer is more exciting!**

Student A and Student B: Compare each pair of sports. Then say
which one you like or think you would like more. Take turns.

hockey/ice skating	cycling/horseback riding
swimming/skiing	volleyball/bowling

I can ask for comparisons.
☐ Very well   ☐ I need more practice.

I can make comparisons.
☐ Very well   ☐ I need more practice.

See Language Booster page 29.

HEALTH

9

10

11

12

REVIEW

ONLINE PRACTICE

31

13 I can write pretty well.

- Describing abilities
- Making recommendations

1 | Vocabulary

A Write the jobs in the categories below. Some may belong to more than one category.

professor	psychologist
nurse	biologist
journalist	surgeon
fashion designer	graphic designer

health	education

arts	science

 B **PAIR WORK** Tell your partner which jobs you think fit in each category.

2 | Conversation

 CD1 **33** **A** Listen. What are Josh and Lily good at? What aren't they good at?

Josh: So, how's school going?

Lily: Well, I'm getting mostly A's and B's. But I'm not doing so well in Portuguese. I'm not very good at languages, I guess.

Josh: No one is good at every subject.

Lily: I suppose. So, are your classes going OK?

Josh: My accounting class is hard. I don't think I'm very good with numbers. But my literature teacher says I'm a good writer.

Lily: You'd make a great journalist.

Josh: As long as I don't write about numbers.

 B **PAIR WORK** Practice the conversation.

CD1 **34** **C** Listen. Write the two extra sentences you hear in the conversation. Practice the new conversation.

pair with **VOCABULARY WORKSHEET 13**

3 | Language Booster

A Notice the different ways we describe abilities and make a recommendation.

Describing abilities	Making a recommendation
I'm good at writing.	
I can write pretty well.	You'd be / You would make | a great journalist.
I'm not very good | with numbers. / at languages.	You should consider becoming / I wouldn't recommend becoming | a teacher.
I can't speak Portuguese very well.	You should get a private tutor.

 B **PAIR WORK** Take turns describing abilities and making recommendations. Use the words from the Vocabulary section.

4 | Pronunciation *Can* and *can't*

CD1 **35** **A** Listen and practice. Notice how we pronounce *can* and *can't*.

/kən/
1. I can read Portuguese.

/kænt/
2. I can't speak Portuguese well.

CD1 **36** **B** Listen. Do you hear *can* or *can't*? Circle the correct words.

1. I *can / can't* speak English.

2. I *can / can't* write well.

3. I *can / can't* use a computer.

4. I *can / can't* understand finance.

 C **PAIR WORK** Practice the sentences in part B. Pay attention to the pronunciation of *can* and *can't*.

ONLINE PRACTICE

SPEAK *with* CONFIDENCE

 A **CLASS ACTIVITY** Talk to five classmates. Find out what they're good at and the kinds of things they can do. Use these ideas and your own ideas.

Are you good at...?		
science	languages	finance
numbers	computers	public speaking
Can you...?		
write	use a computer	work independently
work in a team	meet deadlines	create a spreadsheet

 B **CLASS ACTIVITY** Suggest a good job or a suitable work for each person.

I'd have to have...

1 | Vocabulary

A Look at these jobs. Cross out the word in each group of three that does not fit.

chef	flight attendant	fire fighter
doctor	pop singer	police officer
server	pilot	cashier

 B **PAIR WORK** Tell your partner why the answers you chose do not fit.

Example:

A: A doctor works in a hospital, but a chef and a server work in a restaurant.

2 | Conversation

CD1 37 **A** Listen. What kind of business does Katy want to start? What does she need?

Katy: I want to start my own business after I graduate.

Raul: **Really?**

Katy: I just need to have some money to get started.
And I need to have a fresh idea.

Raul: Do you have any ideas?

Katy: I'd like to sell healthy lunches to people in
offices, things like sandwiches and salads.

Raul: **Do you think it would be difficult to get started?**

Katy: Well, I would need a good kitchen. But I wouldn't have to have a car. I could use a bicycle.

Raul: Good idea.

Katy: Say, I'm looking for a business partner. Are you interested?

 B **PAIR WORK** Practice the conversation. Then exchange the blue and green words above with the
words below and practice it again.

Raul: **That's fantastic!**	Katy: **And a fresh idea is really important.**
Raul: **Would it be hard to get started?**	Katy: **What do you say?**

pair with **VOCABULARY WORKSHEET 14**

3 | Language Booster

A Notice how we express necessity and lack of necessity.

Expressing necessity	**Expressing lack of necessity**	
In business, you need to take risks.	You don't need to have	a car.
I would need a good kitchen.	I wouldn't need to have	an office.
I'd have to have some money.	I wouldn't have to have	
I'd need to have a fresh idea.	I don't have to cook things myself.	

 B PAIR WORK Take turns expressing necessity and lack of necessity for these jobs.

> a translator   an accountant   a writer   an actor

Example:

A: A translator needs to know many languages.

B: Right. You wouldn't have to have an office.

4 | Listening

CD1 **38** **A Listen. Three people are talking to students on *Career Day*. Check (✓) the things they say you need to be successful in these careers.**

A model	A concierge	An architect
☐ to have clear skin	☐ to be friendly	☐ to know interior design
☐ to have healthy hair	☐ to know the area	☐ to be good at math
☐ to be thin	☐ to work late at night	☐ to be able to work alone
☐ to have a college degree	☐ to wear a uniform	☐ to have a license

CD1 **38** **B Listen again. Write one thing each person likes about his or her job.**

1. _____   2. _____   3. _____

ONLINE PRACTICE

SPEAK *with* CONFIDENCE

A PAIR WORK What do you think you need to do to start the businesses below?
Discuss and write your ideas on a piece of paper.

a comic book store

an Internet café

an art gallery

a clothing store

B GROUP WORK Compare your ideas. Does everyone agree?

15 | I travel for free.

• **Describing pros**

• **Describing cons**

1 | Vocabulary

A Look at things that different jobs involve. Mark them **P** (positive) or **N** (negative).

_____ travels for free

_____ works on weekends

_____ makes good money

_____ gets long vacations

_____ stands all day

_____ doesn't need a car

 B **PAIR WORK** Tell your partner positive and negative things about two jobs.

Example:

A: A flight attendant travels for free, but works on weekends.

2 | Conversation

CD1 **39** **A** Listen. What is Keiko's job? What does Keiko like about her new job?

Hi, Keiko. **Are you enjoying your new job?**

Yeah. **So far so good.** I get to meet lots of interesting people.

You're a concierge, right?

Yes. I work for the new hotel downtown.

Do you get to use your language skills?

I do. I use both my French and English.

And how's the salary?

Well, I'm still in training, but **I'll get a raise when I'm done.**

B **PAIR WORK** Practice the conversation. Then exchange the blue and green words above with the words below and practice it again.

Ron: **So, how's it going at work?**   Keiko: **I really like it so far.**

Ron: **And is the salary OK?**   Keiko: **...I'll make more after my training is over.**

36   *pair with* **VOCABULARY WORKSHEET 15**

3 | Language Booster

A Notice how we describe pros and cons.

Describing pros	Describing cons
I get to meet lots of interesting people.	I have to stand all day.
I can use my language skills.	The hours can be long.
I can travel for free.	I don't get much vacation.
I don't have to work weekends.	I don't make much money.

 B **PAIR WORK** Take turns describing the pros and cons of the jobs below.

> a homemaker   a blogger   a flight attendant   a film director

4 | Listening

CD1 **40** **A** Listen to four people talking about their jobs. Circle the correct job.

1. a truck driver / a taxi driver / a bus driver

2. a server / a cashier / a chef

3. a salesclerk / an accountant / an engineer

4. a hair stylist / an art teacher / a pet store manager

CD1 **40** **B** Listen again. Write one thing the people like and one thing they don't like about their jobs. Then compare your answers.

	Likes	Doesn't like
1.		
2.		
3.		
4.		

ONLINE PRACTICE

SPEAK *with* CONFIDENCE

 A **PAIR WORK** Discuss the pros and cons of each job below.

zookeeper   ballet dancer   plumber   candy store owner

 B **GROUP WORK** Discuss which jobs you think are the best or worst.

16 Is the manager there?

• **Asking for someone on the phone**

• **Asking about a job**

1 | Vocabulary

A Which of these things would be important to you when choosing a job? Write VI (very important), SI (somewhat important), or NI (not important).

_____ a company's reputation

_____ salary

_____ location

_____ responsibilities

_____ size of the company

_____ hours

_____ benefits

_____ colleagues

 B **PAIR WORK** Tell your partner a job that interests you. Use the reasons above.

Example:

A: I want to work for Google. The company has a great reputation.

B: I am interested in teaching. The benefits are really good.

2 | Conversation

CD1 **41** **A** Listen. What job is Evan calling about? What experience does the job require?

Manager: Hello. Java Coffee.

Evan: Hello. Can I speak to the manager, please?

Manager: This is the manager.

Evan: Oh, good afternoon. My name is Evan Kincaid. I'm calling about the server position you advertised. Is it still available?

Manager: It is. We haven't filled it yet.

Evan: Great! Can I ask—what are the hours?

Manager: You'd work on weekends only. It's a part-time job.

Evan: That's perfect. And what would my responsibilities be?

Manager: Mostly serving coffee and some light cleaning.

Evan: OK. Do you require any previous experience?

Manager: Not at all. We provide all the training you need. Do you want to come in for an interview?

Evan: Yes! I can come in today!

 B **PAIR WORK** Practice the conversation.

CD1 **42** **C** Listen. Write the two extra sentences you hear in the conversation. Practice the new conversation.

pair with **VOCABULARY WORKSHEET 16**

3 | Language Booster

A Notice the different ways we ask for someone on the phone and ask about a job.

Asking for someone on the phone	Responding
Is the manager there?	This is the manager.
Can I speak to the manager, please?	Speaking.
Could I please speak to the manager?	Please hold. I'll transfer you.

Asking about a job	Responding
Is the job still available?	Yes. We haven't filled it yet.
What would my responsibilities be?	Mostly preparing and serving coffee.
What are the hours?	You'd work on weekends from noon to 5 p.m.

 B **PAIR WORK** Choose one of the jobs below. Take turns asking for the manager and asking about the job.

a private language tutor   a server in a restaurant

4 | Pronunciation Syllable stress

 CD1 **43** **A** Listen and practice. Notice which syllable is stressed in these words.

First syllable	Second syllable	Third syllable
previous	lo**ca**tion	corpo**ra**tion
company	re**qui**re	Japa**ne**se

CD1 **44** **B** Listen and practice. Underline the syllable stressed in each word.

1. manager   2. experience   3. position   4. reputation   5. salary

ONLINE PRACTICE

SPEAK with CONFIDENCE

A You are a manager of a tour company looking for a new guide. Fill in the form below.

Job: Tour guide

Hours: _____

Responsibilities: _____

Salary: _____

Benefits: _____

Necessary experience? _____

B **PAIR WORK** Take turns asking and answering questions about the position.

16

English in Action

ONLINE PRACTICE

1 | Preview

PAIR WORK Casey wants a part-time job. She'd like to work in fashion. Write down the skills you think a person who wants to work in fashion should have.

1. _____   3. _____   5. _____

2. _____   4. _____   6. _____

2 | Practice

A Watch the video. Write the part-time jobs that Maria and Tom suggest to Casey.

1. _____   2. _____   3. _____

B Watch the video again. Each of these sentences contains one error. Correct each one.

1. Casey speaks another language. _____

2. The assistant position starts in a week. _____

3. Casey speaks to the receptionist on the phone. _____

4. The job is four days a week from 9 a.m. to 4 p.m. _____

5. Casey says she writes pretty well and is good with customers. _____

6. Casey talks to the manager of the company. _____

3 | Discuss

GROUP WORK Answer the questions.

1. Do you think Casey will be successful in the job? Why or why not?

2. What are some popular part-time jobs for students?

3. Do you have (or would you like) a part-time job? What is your ideal part-time job?

CONFIDENCE BOOSTER

Student A: Turn to page 85.
Student B: Turn to page 93.

JOBS

13

14

15

16

VIDEO

13 · I can write pretty well.

A Student A: Tell Student B about some things you're good at.

Student B: Suggest a job that you think would be good for Student A.

B Now change roles.

I can describe abilities.
☐ Very well   ☐ I need more practice.

I can make a recommendation.
☐ Very well   ☐ I need more practice.

See Language Booster page 33.

14 · I'd have to have...

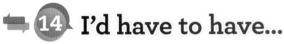

A Student A: Tell Student B what you need in order to be successful in a certain field or job. Include things that are not necessary.

Student B: Listen to Student A and ask follow-up questions.

B Now change roles.

I can express necessity.
☐ Very well   ☐ I need more practice.

I can express lack of necessity.
☐ Very well   ☐ I need more practice.

See Language Booster page 35.

15 · I travel for free.

A Student A: Compare two jobs that might be suitable for you. Describe their pros and cons.

Student B: Listen to Student A and give additional suggestions of your own.

B Now change roles.

I can describe pros.
☐ Very well   ☐ I need more practice.

I can describe cons.
☐ Very well   ☐ I need more practice.

See Language Booster page 37.

16 · Is the manager there?

A Student A: Choose one of the jobs below. "Call" Student B and ask for the manager. Think of and ask three questions about the job.

a magazine editor   a clothing store manager

Student B: You are the manager of the company that Student A is interested in. Answer the phone and answer his or her questions.

B Now change roles.

I can ask for someone on the phone.
☐ Very well   ☐ I need more practice.

I can ask about a job.
☐ Very well   ☐ I need more practice.

See Language Booster page 39.

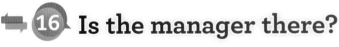

JOBS

13

14

15

16

REVIEW

ONLINE PRACTICE

That sounds fun!

1 | Vocabulary

A What do you like to do in your free time? Rank the actitvities from 1 (most interesting) to 8 (least interesting).

_____ shop   _____ play video games   _____ play sports   _____ sleep in

_____ watch TV   _____ listen to music   _____ chat online   _____ read

B **PAIR WORK** Tell your partner which activities you find most interesting. Which are least interesting?

Example:

A: I think shopping is the most interesting.

B: Not me! I think reading is the most interesting.

2 | Conversation

CD2 ② **A** Listen. What does Steve like to do? What sports does he play?

B **PAIR WORK** Practice the conversation. Then exchange the blue and green words above with the words below.

Steve: **I enjoy reading.**   Ann: **What do you read?**   Steve: **Books, blogs, newspapers...**

3 | Language Booster

A Notice the different ways we ask about free-time activities and show interest.

Asking about free-time activities	Responding	Showing Interest
What do you do / What do you like to do — in your free-time? How do you spend your free-time?	I play sports. I like to play sports. I go to the gym. I enjoy going to the gym.	Oh, yeah? That's interesting. Oh, really? Sounds fun.

 B **PAIR WORK** Take turns asking about and showing interest about free-time activities. Use the ideas below.

in the evening   on the weekend   in the summer

4 | Listening

CD2 ③ **A** Listen. Number the hobbies from 1 to 3 in the order you hear them. There is one extra.

_____ a. photography   _____ b. cooking   _____ c. playing music   _____ d. traveling

CD2 ③ **B** Listen again. Write the names of the people who do the activities.

a. _____ entertains people.   c. _____ gets ideas from the Internet.

b. _____ spends time outdoors.   d. _____ earns extra money.

 C **PAIR WORK** Tell your partner if you spend or earn money with your free time activities.

ONLINE PRACTICE

SPEAK *with* CONFIDENCE

A List three interesting things you like to do in your free time.

1. _____   2. _____   3. _____

 B **CLASS ACTIVITY** Go around the class and find someone who does each thing.

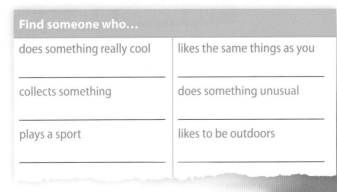

Find someone who...	
does something really cool _____	likes the same things as you _____
collects something _____	does something unusual _____
plays a sport _____	likes to be outdoors _____

What do you do in your free time?

I like to snowboard.

 C **GROUP WORK** Share your information.

18 I'd love to go.

1 | Vocabulary

A What kinds of movies do you like? Circle your three favorite kinds of movies.

comedies   thrillers   romantic comedies   historical dramas

animated movies   horror films   action movies   science fiction movies

 B **PAIR WORK** Ask and answer questions about movies you like and don't like. Use the words above.

Examples:

A: What movie genres do you like?   **B:** What kinds of movies don't you like?

B: I love action movies and comedies.   **A:** I don't really like horror films.

2 | Conversation

CD2 **4** **A** Listen. What movie will Jeff and Kirk see? What will they do after the movie?

 Jeff: Hey Kirk, do you have plans for Friday night?

 Kirk: Friday night? I don't think so. Why?

 Jeff: Do you want to see a movie?

 Kirk: Sure, I'd love to. What's playing?

 Jeff: *Free Fall* is playing at the theater.

 Kirk: Great! I love action movies.

When do you want to meet?

 Jeff: How about at 7 p.m., in front of the theater?

 Kirk: OK. And let's get some pizza after the movie.

 Jeff: Sounds good. See you then!

FREE FALL

Now playing in theaters.

 B **PAIR WORK** Practice the conversation.

CD2 **5** **C** Listen. Write the two extra sentences you hear in the conversation. Practice the new conversation.

3 | Language Booster

A Notice the different ways we invite someone and respond to an invitation.

Inviting someone		Responding to an invitation
Do you want to Would you like to	see a movie?	I'd love to. Sounds great. Sure. /OK. Maybe./I'm not sure.

 B **PAIR WORK** Take turns inviting and responding to invitations. Use the ideas below.

go shopping   go to a karaoke bar   go to a theme park   go to a concert

4 | Pronunciation   Reduction of *want to*

CD2 **6** **A** Listen and practice. Notice how *want to* is reduced to /wanna/.

A: Do you want to see a movie?

B: OK. That sounds great. I really want to see the new Johnny Depp movie.

 B **PAIR WORK** Ask and answer three questions that begin with *Do you want to…?* Reduce *want to*.

ONLINE PRACTICE

SPEAK *with* CONFIDENCE

A **CLASS ACTIVITY** Read the ads. Choose three activities and invite three people to do them with you.

WHAT'S ON? | Your guide to weekend events

Luciano's Pizza
Open from 11 a.m.
20% off between
3 p.m. and 6 p.m. all weekend.

Mega Mall
Biggest sale of the year!
Open 24 hours this
weekend.

Rock the Park Sunday!
Local rock bands play.
Starts at 1 p.m. at City Park.

Windgate Art Museum
Picasso in Paris exhibit.
Saturday 10 p.m.–5 p.m.
Closed Sundays.

Love is the Answer
See the romantic comedy
everyone's talking about!
Shows at 7 p.m. and 9:30 p.m.

Adventureland Park
Try out latest roller coaster—
the Death Scream!
Open till midnight Friday.

Teresa, do you want to go to a concert on Sunday?

Sure, I'd love to. What time do you want to meet?

Let's meet at the park at 12:30.

B **CLASS ACTIVITY** With a partner, present your choice to the class. What is the most popular activity?

I'm sorry, but I can't.

1 | Vocabulary

A How often do you go to these places? Write P (pretty often), H (hardly ever), or N (never).

_____ coffee shop   _____ mall   _____ beach   _____ movie theater   _____ library

_____ museum   _____ pool   _____ park   _____ theme park   _____ bookstore

B   PAIR WORK   Tell your partner how often you go to the places above.

Example:

A: I go to the movie theater pretty often.

B: I hardly ever go. I watch movies at home. I go to the mall pretty often.

2 | Conversation

CD2 **7   A   Listen. Why can't Beth go to the museum? Why can't Chen go tomorrow?**

Beth: Hello?

Chen: Beth? Hi, it's Chen.

Beth: Hi! How's everything?

Chen: Great. **Listen, would you like to go to the museum later?**

Beth: I'm sorry, but I can't.

Chen: Really? Why not?

Beth: **I have to go to work.** Do you want to go tomorrow? I'm off then.

Chen: I'd love to, but I can't. **I'm going to the mall with my brother.**

Beth: Oh, I see...**what about the weekend?**

Chen: I can go Saturday.

Beth: Me too!

Chen: Sounds good. Let's grab a bite before we go.

Beth: OK! Sounds perfect.

Chen: See you soon!

B   PAIR WORK   Practice the conversation. Then exchange the blue and green words above with the words below and practice it again.

Chen: **Do you want to go to the bookstore?**   Beth: **I need to study.**   Chen: **I have soccer practice.**

Beth: **... are you free this weekend?**

3 | Language Booster

A Notice the different ways we decline an invitation and give an excuse.

Declining an invitation	Giving an excuse	Responding
Sorry.	I have to go to work.	
I'm really sorry.	I need to do my homework.	Oh, I see.
I'd love to, but I can't.	I want to clean my room.	Oh, that's OK.
I'm afraid I can't.	I'd like to go to the gym.	

 B **PAIR WORK** Take turns inviting each other to the places in the Vocabulary section. Decline the invitations and give excuses.

4 | Listening

CD2 **8** **A** Listen. Number the invitations from 1 to 4 in the order you hear them.

_____ a. eat fast food   _____ b. see a movie   _____ c. go to the mall   _____ d. play video games

CD2 **8** **B** Listen again. Do people accept or decline? Circle your answers. When someone declines an invitation, write the excuse.

1. accept / decline: _____   3. accept / decline: _____

2. accept / decline: _____   4. accept / decline: _____

C **PAIR WORK** Compare answers with a partner.

ONLINE PRACTICE

SPEAK *with* CONFIDENCE

A Check (✓) two things you want to do this weekend. Write excuses for the things you don't want to do.

Things to do	Excuses
☐ go to the beach	
☐ go to the mall	
☐ go out to dinner	
☐ play video games	
☐ go to the park	

B **CLASS ACTIVITY** Invite people to do things. Decline some invitations.

• **Apologizing**

• **Responding to an apology**

1 | Vocabulary

A Look at these six excuses for being late. Complete them with the correct words from the box.

| broke down | stuck in | ran into | lost track | needed to | couldn't find |

1. I _____ run an errand first.

2. I was _____ traffic.

3. My car _____.

4. I _____ an old friend.

5. I _____ my keys.

6. I completely _____ of the time.

 B PAIR WORK Take turns asking your partner why he or she is late and giving excuses.

Example:

A: Why are you late?

B: There was a lot of traffic.

2 | Conversation

CD2 **9** **A** Listen. Why is Lisa late? When will she arrive?

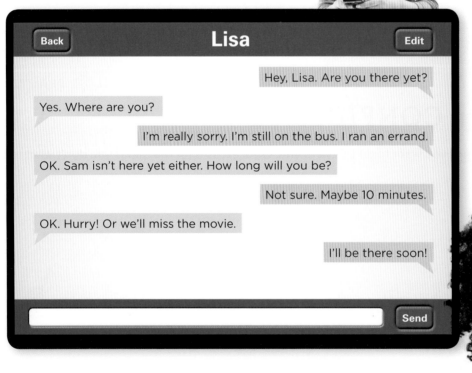

| Back | **Lisa** | Edit |

Hey, Lisa. Are you there yet?

Yes. Where are you?

I'm really sorry. I'm still on the bus. I ran an errand.

OK. Sam isn't here yet either. How long will you be?

Not sure. Maybe 10 minutes.

OK. Hurry! Or we'll miss the movie.

I'll be there soon!

| | Send |

 B PAIR WORK Practice the conversation.

CD2 **10** **C** Listen. Write the two extra sentences you hear in the conversation. Practice the new conversation.

3 | Language Booster

A Notice how we apologize and respond to an apology.

Apologizing		Responding to an apology
Sorry I'm sorry I'm really sorry I'm so sorry	I'm late. I got stuck in traffic.	Oh, that's OK. No problem. Don't worry about it.

 B **PAIR WORK** Take turns apologizing and responding to apologies. Use the ideas below.

> I had to walk my dog.   I ran into a friend.   I lost track of the time.

4 | Pronunciation Using stress and duration to convey emotion

CD2 ⓫ **A** Listen to three people say they are sorry. Which one is not really sorry?

A: Oh, Jun. I'm **so** sorry!

B: I'm **sorry** I'm late again. I really have a good excuse this time.

C: Well, **sorry**! I didn't think you'd mind.

 B **PAIR WORK** Practice the conversation above. Pay attention to correct stress.

> ONLINE PRACTICE

SPEAK with CONFIDENCE

A Write an excuse and a response for each conversation.

A: Where have you been? I've been here for an hour!

B: _____

A: _____

A: I missed you at my party last night. I was hoping to see you there.

B: _____

A: _____

 B **PAIR WORK** Take turns practicing the conversations.
Decide if your partner is really sorry or not.

> Where have you been? I've been here for an hour!
>
> I'm sorry I'm late. I was stuck in traffic.
>
> That's OK. You're here now.

 C **CLASS ACTIVITY** Present one conversation to the class.

49

English in Action

1 | Preview

 PAIR WORK Look at the pictures. What do you think happens? Put them in order from 1 to 4.

2 | Practice

A Watch the video. Check your guesses in the Preview section. Did you guess correctly?

B Watch the video again. Answer the questions.

1. What is Eric learning to play? _____.

2. What are Eric, Casey, and Jill doing tonight? _____.

3. Has Maria seen Jill? What did Jill say to Maria? _____.

4. Does Maria go to the movies with Casey and Eric? _____.

5. What excuses does Jill give for being late? _____.

3 | Discuss

GROUP WORK Answer the questions.

1. How often are you late? What do you do when you are late?

2. Are there any excuses that make it OK to be late? What are they?

CONFIDENCE BOOSTER Student A: Turn to page 86.
Student B: Turn to page 94.

FREE TIME

17

18

19

20

VIDEO

17 That sounds fun!

A Student A: Ask Student B what he or she likes to do on weekends. Show interest and ask follow-up questions.

   Student B: Answer Student A's questions. Include at least three things you like to do.

B Now change roles.

I can ask/talk about free-time activities.
☐ Very well   ☐ I need more practice.

I can show interest.
☐ Very well   ☐ I need more practice.

See Language Booster page 43.

18 I'd love to go.

A Student A: Invite Student B to do three fun things with you this weekend.

   Student B: Accept each of Student A's invitations. Ask for more information.

B Now change roles.

I can invite someone to do something.
☐ Very well   ☐ I need more practice.

I can respond to an invitation.
☐ Very well   ☐ I need more practice.

See Language Booster page 45.

19 I'm sorry, but I can't.

A Student A: Invite Student B to do three things with you this weekend.

   Student B: Decline each of Student A's invitations. Give an excuse for each one.

B Now change roles.

I can decline an invitation.
☐ Very well   ☐ I need more practice.

I can give an excuse.
☐ Very well   ☐ I need more practice.

See Language Booster page 47.

20 Sorry I'm late.

A Student A: Apologize to Student B for being late. Add an excuse.

   Student B: Acknowledge Student A's apology.

B Now change roles.

I can apologize.
☐ Very well   ☐ I need more practice.

I can respond to an apology.
☐ Very well   ☐ I need more practice.

See Language Booster page 49.

ONLINE PRACTICE

21 Did you go alone?

1 | Vocabulary

A Look at the things you can do when you visit a new place. Check (✓) the activities you like to do.

_____ go shopping   _____ visit markets   _____ take tours

_____ try local food   _____ go to the theater   _____ see sporting events

_____ go to museums   _____ take photos   _____ see historical sights

B **PAIR WORK** Tell your partner the things you like to do when you travel.

Example:

A: I like to go shopping when I visit a new place. What about you?

B: I like to take photos.

2 | Conversation

 CD2 ⑫ **A** Listen. Who did Reiko travel to Hong Kong with? What did she think of Hong Kong Disneyland?

Mark: So, where did you go for vacation?

Reiko: I went to Hong Kong.

Mark: Wow! Who did you go with? Did you go alone?

Reiko: No, I traveled with my sister.

Mark: How fun! And what did you do there?
Did you go to Victoria Peak?

Reiko: Yeah, we also took a city tour. I took a lot of photos.

Mark: I can't wait to see them. Did you go to Hong Kong Disneyland?

Reiko: We did. It's small, but it's nice. Oh, and I went shopping.

Mark: Of course. And what did you buy me?

B **PAIR WORK** Practice the conversation.

CD2 ⑬ **C** Listen. Write the two extra sentences you hear in the conversation. Practice the new conversation.

3 | Language Booster

A Notice how we ask double questions and describe past events.

Asking double questions	Describing past events
Where did you go for vacation? Did you go anywhere special?	Yeah, I did. I went to Hong Kong.
Who did you go with? Did you go alone?	No, I traveled with my sister.
What did you do there? Did you go to Victoria Peak?	Yeah, we went to the top. We also took a city tour.
How was the weather? Was it sunny?	It was OK. It was rainy for some of the time.

 B **PAIR WORK** Write three sets of double questions to ask about a recent trip. Take turns asking your questions.

Example:

A: Where did you go on your last trip? Did you go anywhere fun?

B: I did. I went camping with some friends.

4 | Pronunciation   Reduction of *did you*

CD2 **14** **A** Listen and practice. Notice how we pronounce *did you* in *wh-* questions.

/Who'ja/
1. Who did you travel with?

/Wha'ja/
2. What did you do there?

/Where'ja/
3. Where did you go?

/When'ja/
4. When did you get back?

/Why'ja/
5. Why did you go there?

/How'ja/
6. How did you travel?

 B **PAIR WORK** Practice the questions above with a new partner. Pay attention to the reduction of *did you*.

ONLINE PRACTICE

SPEAK *with* CONFIDENCE

GROUP WORK Take turns describing an interesting trip you took. Ask the questions below and add a second question to make double questions.

Who did you go with?   Where did you stay?

When did you go?   What did you do there?

How did you get there?   How was the weather?

Which do you prefer?

- **Asking about preferences**
- **Describing preferences**

1 | Vocabulary

A Look at these different vacation options. Mark ✓ if you want to try it and ✗ if you don't.

_____ a camping trip   _____ a backpacking trip   _____ an adventure holiday

_____ a cruise   _____ a spa resort   _____ a bus tour

 B **PAIR WORK** Tell your partner which options you want to try. Give reasons.

Example:

A: I'd like to go on a camping trip. I love to be outdoors.

B: It's not for me. It doesn't sound fun.

2 | Conversation

CD2 **15** **A** **Listen. Why does Annie prefer hostels? What tour does Jill suggest?**

So Jill, I have my plane ticket to Munich. **I just need to decide what to do there.**

Maybe I can help, Annie. Do you prefer traveling alone or in a group?

1

I prefer traveling in a group. I usually have more fun with other people.

And which would you prefer—staying in hostels or staying in hotels?

2

I'd prefer staying in hostels. **It's easier to meet people in hostels.**

That's true. And would you rather travel by bus or train?

3

I'd rather travel by train.

OK. Then how about this six-day train tour of Bavaria? **Each night you have a choice of a hotel or a hostel.**

4

 B **PAIR WORK** Practice the conversation. Then exchange the blue and green words above with the words below and practice it again.

Annie: **Now it's time to decide what kind of trip I want.**   Jill: Let me see if I can help.

Annie: **I can save a lot of money that way.**   Jill: You make your own hostel arrangements.

3 | Language Booster

A Notice the different ways we ask about and describe preferences.

Asking about preferences	Describing preferences
Do you prefer traveling alone or in a group?	I prefer traveling in a group (to traveling alone).
Which would you prefer—staying in hostels or staying in hotels?	I'd prefer staying in hostels (to staying in hotels).
Would you rather travel by bus or train?	I'd rather travel by train (than travel by bus).

 B **PAIR WORK** Look at these tourist options. Ask and answer questions about your preferences.

going on a camping trip/going to a resort spa   taking a cruise/taking a backpacking trip

4 | Listening

CD2 **16** **A** Listen. Two friends are planning a vacation. Circle their preferences.

Preference	Reason
1. backpacking trip / eco-tour	They would rather _____.
2. bus / train	They prefer _____.
3. hotels / hostels	They want to _____.
4. restaurant meals / street food	They prefer _____.

CD2 **16** **B** Listen again. Why did they decide on each choice? Complete the reasons.

ONLINE PRACTICE

SPEAK *with* CONFIDENCE

A Look at this survey. Check (✓) your travel preferences.

WHAT KIND OF TRAVELER ARE YOU?		
I prefer traveling with...	**I would rather eat...**	**I would rather...**
_____ a friend. _____ a group.	_____ local food. _____ familiar food.	_____ plan each day in advance. _____ just see what happens.
I would rather stay in...	**I would rather...**	**I would prefer visiting...**
_____ hostels. _____ hotels.	_____ start the day early. _____ sleep in and going out later.	_____ unusual places. _____ the main tourist attractions.
I prefer...		
_____ shopping. _____ visiting museums.		

 B **GROUP WORK** Interview three classmates. Who would be a good person to travel with?

23 You must get a visa.

- **Expressing prohibitions**
- **Expressing obligations**

1 | Vocabulary

A Look at these items people sometimes pack for a trip. Circle the ones you would definitely take on an overseas trip.

a lock   a travel pillow   a first-aid kit   an electricity adaptor

medicine   a passport   a hair dryer   a portable stove

 **B** **PAIR WORK** Tell your partner what you take when you travel. Use the words above and your own ideas.

Example:

A: I take medicine just in case I get sick. What do you definitely take?

B: I always bring a travel pillow.

2 | Conversation

CD2 **17** **A** Listen. What does Miguel need to buy? What did he almost forget?

Teresa: Did you pack everything you need?

Miguel: Uh-huh. I just need to buy a travel pillow at the airport.

Teresa: So, this is your first overseas trip *and* your first flight! Are you nervous?

Miguel: Not at all.

Teresa: Remember, you're not allowed to take liquids on the plane.

Miguel: Really? OK. I hope I didn't forget anything.

Teresa: You must take your passport!

Miguel: Oh, of course. I guess I am a little nervous!

 B **PAIR WORK** Practice the conversation.

CD2 **18** **C** Listen. Write the two extra sentences you hear in the conversation. Practice the new conversation.

3 | Language Booster

A Notice the different ways we express prohibitions and obligations.

Expressing prohibitions		Expressing obligations	
You can't	travel without a passport.	You must	take your passport.
You're not allowed to	take liquids on a plane.	You have to	pack liquids.
You're not permitted to	check three bags.	I need to	buy a travel pillow.
		You don't have to	leave until 2 p.m.

 B PAIR WORK Take turns expressing prohibitions and obligations for a camping trip. Use the words in the Vocabulary section and your own ideas.

Example:

A: We have to pack a first-aid kit.

B: We're not permitted to bring a portable stove.

4 | Pronunciation Reduction of *have to* and *has to*

CD2 **19** **A** Listen and practice. Notice how *have to* is pronounced *hafta* and *has to* is pronounced *hasta*.

1. We don't have to pack a hair dryer.　　2. She has to pack a first-aid kit.

 B PAIR WORK Your class is planning a hiking trip in the mountains. Make sentences using *have to* and *has to* with the ideas below. Pay attention to the reduction of *have to* and *has to*.

be on time	bring lots of clothes	pack a tent	pack a hair dryer

ONLINE PRACTICE

SPEAK *with* CONFIDENCE

 A PAIR WORK Look at these signs you might see while traveling. What do you think they mean?

> This one means you must stop.

 B CLASS ACTIVITY Create your own sign and show it to the class. Be creative! Who can guess what it means?

24 # When is the next train?

• **Asking about prices and schedules**

• **Describing prices and schedules**

1 | Vocabulary

A Look at these words related to travel. Which word in each set doesn't belong? Cross it out.

1. fare ~~luggage~~ price
2. one-way terminal round trip
3. flight depart arrive
4. station ticket airport
5. gate first class platform
6. train boarding pass subway

 B PAIR WORK Compare with a partner. Give reasons why you crossed out the words.

Example:

A: Fare and price are the cost of a ticket. Luggage is a bag.

2 | Conversation

CD2 **20** **A** Listen. Is a train leaving after 7:15 p.m.? How long does the trip to New York City take?

 Tourist: Hello. **How much is a one-way ticket to New York City?**

 Agent: **It's $86.50.**

 Tourist: And when is the next train?

 Agent: It leaves at 7:15 p.m. **That's the last train of the day.**

 Tourist: OK. How long does it take to get there?

 Agent: About three hours. It arrives at 10:20 p.m.

 Tourist: **And where does it depart from?**

 Agent: Platform four. Would you like a ticket? The train is leaving soon.

 B PAIR WORK Practice the conversation. Then exchange the blue and green words above with the words below and practice it again.

Tourist: **What does a one-way ticket to New York City cost?** ▷ Agent: **The price is $86.50 plus tax.**

Agent: **After that, there's no other train until tomorrow.** ▷ Tourist: **Where does the train leave from?**

3 | Language Booster

A Notice how we talk about prices and schedules.

Asking about prices and schedules	Describing prices and schedules
How much is a one-way/round trip ticket to New York?	It's $86.50. The price is $86.50 plus tax.
When is the next train to New York?	It leaves at 7:15 p.m.
How long does it take?	It takes about three hours.
Where does the train from Chicago arrive?	It arrives at Platform four.
What gate does the flight to Miami depart from?	It departs from Gate 58.

 B PAIR WORK Choose two places you can get to by bus. Take turns asking and answering questions about prices and schedules.

4 | Listening

 CD2 **21** **A** Listen. Number the places from 1 to 3 in the order you hear them. There is one extra.

_____ a. a subway station   _____ b. a bus station   _____ c. a train station   _____ d. an airport

CD2 **21** **B** Listen again. Complete the sentences. Then compare answers with a partner.

1. The ticket to Paris costs _____ pounds. The trip takes _____ hours.

2. The tourist is leaving from _____ 16. She needs to _____ in Mexico City.

3. The tourist will get to Ottawa at _____ p.m. The agent doesn't know the _____.

 ONLINE PRACTICE

SPEAK *with* CONFIDENCE

A PAIR WORK Student A is the ticket agent who has the information below. Student B is a tourist and asks Student A for ticketing information for the next train from Barcelona to Madrid.

Next train from Barcelona to Madrid

| Ticket:
 117 euros (one-way) | Departure:
 5:00 p.m. | Travel time:
 2 hours 45 minutes |
| Direct or transfer:
 Direct | Depart:
 Platform 16 | Arrive:
 Platform 2 |

0052737645

B PAIR WORK Now switch roles. Use the information below.

NEXT FLIGHT FROM SINGAPORE TO BANGKOK   TICKET

| Ticket:
 68 Singapore dollars | Departure:
 7:30 a.m. | Travel time:
 45 minutes | 07824100341 |
| Direct or transfer:
 Direct | Depart:
 Gate 44C | Arrive:
 Gate 39 | |

English in Action

ONLINE PRACTICE

1 | Preview

PAIR WORK Tom is sharing his Australian vacation photos with Casey. Tell your partner which places you want to visit. Give reasons.

TRAVEL

21
22
23
24

VIDEO

a

b

Kakadu National Park

c

Great Barrier Reef

d

Sydney Harbor

2 | Practice

A Watch the video. Number the photos from 1 to 3 in the order that Tom visited the places.

B Watch the video again. Check (✓) the questions you hear.

1. ☐ How long did you stay there?　　☐ How long were you there?

2. ☐ What places did you visit?　　☐ Did you visit many places?

3. ☐ How was the weather there?　　☐ What was the weather like there?

4. ☐ Did you get around by bus?　　☐ Did you travel by bus?

3 | Discuss

GROUP WORK Answer the questions.

1. What do you like about Tom's trip to Australia?

2. Where would you like to go on vacation? Would you stay in your country or go overseas?

3. Was there a place you visited and really enjoyed? Describe the place and the things you did.

ⒸONFIDENCE BOOSTER　Student A: Turn to page 87.
Student B: Turn to page 95.

 21 ## Did you go alone?

A Student A: Ask Student B questions about a weekend trip he or she took. Ask three sets of double questions.

Student B: Answer Student A's questions.

B Now change roles.

I can ask double questions.
☐ Very well ☐ I need more practice.

I can describe past events.
☐ Very well ☐ I need more practice.

See Language Booster page 53.

 22 ## Which do you prefer?

Student A and Student B: Find out about each other's dream vacation. Ask about preferences on two of the ideas below.

| where to travel | when to travel | transportation | places to stay |

I can ask about preferences.
☐ Very well ☐ I need more practice.

I can describe preferences.
☐ Very well ☐ I need more practice.

See Language Booster page 55.

 23 ## You must get a visa.

A Student A: Student B is a foreign visitor. Say two things that he or she is not allowed to do, and two things that he or she has to do while visiting your country.

Student B: You are a foreign visitor. Listen to Student A and ask follow-up questions.

B Now change roles.

I can express prohibition.
☐ Very well ☐ I need more practice.

I can express obligation.
☐ Very well ☐ I need more practice.

See Language Booster page 57.

 24 ## When is the next train?

A Student A: You are a bus ticket agent. Create your own bus ticket like the tickets on page 65. Student B is a tourist. Answer his or her questions.

Student B: Ask for the information from Student A's bus ticket.

B Now change roles.

I can ask about prices and schedules.
☐ Very well ☐ I need more practice.

I can describe prices and schedules.
☐ Very well ☐ I need more practice.

See Language Booster page 59.

ONLINE PRACTICE

I usually wear...

1 | Vocabulary

A **Circle the clothes you are wearing now.**

a suit   a dress shirt   a scarf   a skirt   a dress   a uniform

a T-shirt   sandals   shorts   running shoes   jeans

 B **PAIR WORK** **Tell your partner how you usually dress. Use the words above or your own ideas.**

Example:

A: I usually wear jeans, a T-shirt, and running shoes.

B: I often wear khakis and a dress shirt.

2 | Conversation

CD2 **22** **A** **Listen. What is a kilt? When do Scottish men wear it?**

 Susan: The music is great, and I love your clothes. Are they traditional?

 Calum: Oh, yes. You probably know this—it's called a kilt.

 Susan: Yeah. I've seen them in pictures. Is it a kind of skirt?

 Calum: Well, Scottish men don't really call it a *skirt*. People usually
wear it on special occasions.

 Susan: I see. I love the pattern.

 Calum: The pattern is plaid. Scotland is famous for them. The pattern can tell you what
family someone is from.

 Susan: How interesting! Is there a traditional outfit for women as well?

 Calum: Yes. Women normally wear longer skirts. But when they dance, they may wear
kilts. I think there will be a women's dance performance later.

 B **PAIR WORK** **Practice the conversation.**

CD2 **23** **C** **Listen. Write the two extra sentences you hear in the conversation. Practice the new conversation.**

3 | Language Booster

A Notice the different ways we talk about general behavior.

Asking about general behavior	Describing general behavior
What do Scottish people generally wear to weddings?	They generally wear a kilt.
What do women in Scotland normally wear?	They normally wear a long skirt, but they sometimes wear a kilt, too.
How do teachers tend to dress at your school?	Men wear slacks, a shirt, and a tie. Women tend to wear a blouse, a skirt, and a jacket.

 B **PAIR WORK** Choose four items of clothing from the Vocabulary section. When or where do people generally wear them? Take turns asking and answering questions.

Examples:

A: Where do people generally wear sandals?

B: They normally wear them to the beach. When do women normally wear dresses?

4 | Pronunciation Intonation in a series of things

CD2 24 **A** Listen and practice. Notice the intonation when we say a series of things.

1. Men wear slacks, | a shirt, | and a tie.
2. Women tend to wear a blouse, | a skirt, | and a jacket.

 B **PAIR WORK** Take turns describing what men and women generally wear to work in offices in your country. Pay attention to your intonation.

ONLINE PRACTICE

SPEAK *with* CONFIDENCE

 A **PAIR WORK** What do people generally wear on these occasions? Is it different for men and women? What about for teenagers and adults?

graduation day	a classical music concert
a wedding	a job interview

What do girls generally wear on graduation day?

They usually wear nice dresses.

 B **GROUP WORK** Choose one of the occasions in part A. What do people normally do on this occasion?

26 What do you think?

• Asking for ideas

• Offering ideas

1 | Vocabulary

A How important are these things when you choose clothes? Mark ✓ (important) or ✗ (not very important).

_____ brand _____ design _____ material _____ value

_____ quality _____ price _____ color _____ comfort

 B **PAIR WORK** Tell your partner what's important and not important when you buy clothes.

Examples:

A: For me, brand is very important. How about you?

B: It's not important at all. Quality is the most important to me.

2 | Conversation

CD2 **25** **A** Listen. Why doesn't Ana care for the first jacket? Do you think the last jacket suits Tom?

B **PAIR WORK** Practice the conversation. Then exchange the blue and green words above with the words below and practice it again.

Tom: **Can I wear something like this?** ⫶⟩ **Is this a good color on me?**

Ana: **Um...maybe you could look at a different color.** ⫶⟩ **I found the perfect jacket for you!**

64   *pair with* VOCABULARY WORKSHEET 26

3 | Language Booster

A Notice how we ask for and offer ideas.

Asking for ideas	Offering ideas
What do you think?	I would get something more practical.
Do you think this design is nice?	A different design might be better.
Is this a good color for me?	You might want to try a different color.
Do you think this looks good on me?	I think this will look better on you.

B You are shopping for a new outfit. Check (✓) the items you would buy.

Pants	Belt	Shirt	Shoes	Socks
☐ baggy yellow	☐ black leather	☐ pink with purple flowers	☐ red running shoes	☐ dark blue

 C PAIR WORK Take turns asking for and offering ideas for the items you checked.

4 | Listening

CD2 26 **A** Listen to four conversations. Which item of clothing is each speaker discussing? Number them from 1 to 4.

 a

 b

 c

 d

CD2 26 **B** Listen again. Write the idea that is offered in each conversation.

1. _____   3. _____

2. _____   4. _____

ONLINE PRACTICE

SPEAK with CONFIDENCE

 PAIR WORK The people in the picture want a different look. Take turns asking for and offering ideas.

I think she should try different glasses.

I would get something more colorful.

I agree...

Can you do me a favor?

• Making requests

• Agreeing to requests

1 | Vocabulary

A Look at the picture. Write the correct number of the item in the picture.

1. a rug   3. a clock   5. a vase   7. a lamp

2. a mirror   4. pillows   6. candles   8. curtains

 B **PAIR WORK** Tell your partner what new objects you would like to have.

Example:

A: I want a new mirror for my bedroom.

B: I want new curtains.

A: Me too! What color do you want to get?

2 | Conversation

CD2 27 **A** Listen. What did Jake and Ben look at online? What does Ben ask Jake to get at the store?

Jake: Hello.

Ben: Hi, Jake. It's me, Ben. Are you still at the home decor store?

Jake: Yeah, I just found the lamp we looked at online.
It will look great in our new apartment.

Ben: Oh, good. Listen, can you do me a favor?

Jake: Sure.

Ben: Would you get some pillows for the sofa?

Jake: No problem. Do you want any particular color?

Ben: How about green?

Jake: Sure. Anything else?

Ben: Would you mind picking up a mirror, too?

Jake: Not at all. Do we need anything else?

Ben: Actually...can you pick up some food? Our fridge is empty.

 B **PAIR WORK** Practice the conversation.

CD2 28 **C** Listen. Write the two extra sentences you hear in the conversation. Practice the new conversation.

3 | Language Booster

A Notice the different ways we make and agree to requests.

Making requests	Agreeing to requests
Would you / Could you please — get some pillows for the sofa?	Sure. No problem.
Would you/Do you mind picking up a mirror?	Of course. I'd be happy to.
Can you do me a favor?	No, I don't mind.

B **PAIR WORK** Take turns making a request and agreeing to a request. Use the ideas below.

Can you show me…?	Would you tell me the price of…?
Could you please hand me…?	Would you mind looking for a different…?

4 | Pronunciation Reduction of *would you* and *could you*

 A Listen and practice. Notice how *would you* and *could you* are reduced.

/wouldja/
1. Would you get some pillows?

/couldja/
2. Could you please pick up some plants?

B **PAIR WORK** Take turns making requests. Pay attention to the reduction of *could you* and *would you*.

ONLINE PRACTICE

SPEAK *with* CONFIDENCE

PAIR WORK Look at the room below. You and your partner are roommates. Take turns making requests to fix the room and agreeing to the request.

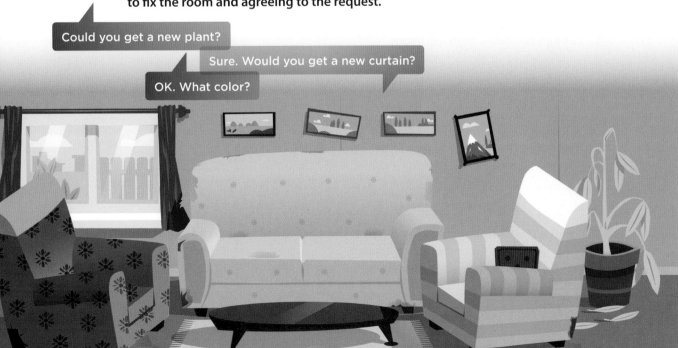

Could you get a new plant?

Sure. Would you get a new curtain?

OK. What color?

28 What is it used for?

• Asking about uses

• Describing uses

1 | Vocabulary

A Look at the things that people can do on their smartphones. Circle the things you or your friends do on your smartphones.

read books	video chat	get directions	play games
watch movies	store photos	check the weather	send e-mails

 B **PAIR WORK** Tell your partner which ones you prefer to do on a computer.

Examples:

A: I prefer to use my computer to send e-mails.

B: I like to get directions on my computer. The maps are too small on smartphones.

2 | Conversation

CD2 30 **A** Listen. What does Dave mostly use his new tablet for? What does he think is the most useful feature?

Dave: Hi, Helena. Are you busy?

Helena: Not really. **What you are doing?**

Dave: I'm playing with my new tablet. **I just got it.**

Helena: I need to get one of those. They're so cool looking. What do you use it for?

Dave: Lots of things. I mostly use it to store photos and watch movies. **It's so much better than my phone.**

Helena: **What is its most interesting feature?**

Dave: The most useful feature is probably the editing software. I can use it for recording, editing, and sharing my own music.

Helena: How fun!

 B **PAIR WORK** Practice the conversation. Then exchange the blue and green words above with the words below and practice it again.

Helena: **What are you up to?** ⟶ Dave: **It was a birthday present.**

Dave: **I prefer this to my phone.** ⟶ Helena: **What feature do you like the best?**

3│Language Booster

A Notice the different ways we ask about and describe uses.

Asking about uses	Describing uses
What do you use it for?	I use it to store photos and watch movies.
How can you use it?	I can use it to read books and do homework.
What is it used for?	It's used for recording, editing, and sharing my music.
What is its most interesting feature?	The most useful feature is the editing software.

 B **PAIR WORK** Take turns asking about and describing the uses of the things below.

a scanner   a GPS   a microwave oven   a camera

4│Listening

 A Listen. Number each product from 1–4 in the order you hear. Write one use for each product.

_____   _____   _____   _____

B Listen again. Write the price for each product.

1. Electric Guitar Bag: _____

2. Panda Chopsticks: _____

3. Wrongulator: _____

4. Clone Doll: _____

ONLINE PRACTICE

SPEAK *with* CONFIDENCE

 A **PAIR WORK** Design a perfect household robot. Think of five things you can use it for. Compare features and choose the best ones.

My robot does the laundry and folds everything just the way I like.

Mine can read books and help me study for tests!

B **CLASS ACTIVITY** Present your features. Vote on who has the coolest robot.

English in Action

1 | Preview

 PAIR WORK Casey is packing for her trip to Australia. Look at the items her friends give her. Tell your partner which items you think Casey needs.

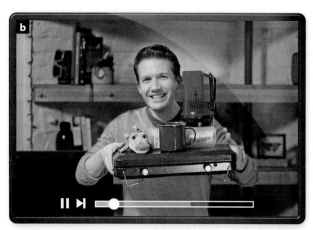

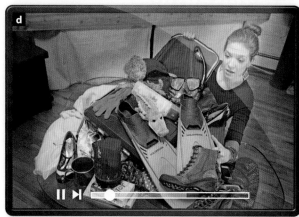

2 | Practice

A PAIR WORK Watch the video. List the things that Casey's friends lend her. Then compare with a partner.

B Watch the video again. Look at the statements below. Mark the statements T (true) or F (false).

_____ 1. Casey likes to pack light.

_____ 2. Eric has a tablet for Casey to borrow.

_____ 3. Tom recommends that Casey bring a first-aid kit.

_____ 4. Jill lends Casey some boots.

_____ 5. Casey asks to borrow Tom's books.

3 | Discuss

GROUP WORK Answer the questions.

1. What things do you need to bring with you when you travel?

2. Are there things that you think are made best in your country? What?

3. Do you usually travel light or pack more then you need? Why?

CONFIDENCE BOOSTER

Student A: Turn to page 88.
Student B: Turn to page 96.

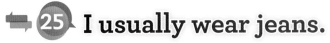

25 I usually wear jeans.

A **Student A:** Ask Student B what young people normally wear in his or her town to go to school. Ask follow-up questions.

Student B: Answer Student A's questions.

B Now change roles. Student B asks Student A what people in his or her town normally wear on formal occasions.

I can ask about general behavior.
☐ Very well ☐ I need more practice.

I can describe general behavior.
☐ Very well ☐ I need more practice.

See Language Booster page 63.

26 What do you think?

A **Student A:** Choose two of these items. Tell Student B you're thinking of buying them. Ask what he or she thinks.

used shoes for $200	a black T-shirt for $100
an orange suit for $30	a pair of pink sunglasses

Student B: Listen to what Student A is thinking of buying. Offer other ideas.

B Now change roles.

I can ask for ideas.
☐ Very well ☐ I need more practice.

I can offer ideas.
☐ Very well ☐ I need more practice.

See Language Booster page 65.

27 Can you do me a favor?

A **Student A:** Think of three things you'd like Student B to do for you. Make three requests.

Student B: Agree to Student A's requests.

B Now change roles.

I can make requests.
☐ Very well ☐ I need more practice.

I can agree to requests.
☐ Very well ☐ I need more practice.

See Language Booster page 67.

28 What is it used for?

A **Student A:** Choose a gadget or household item that you often use. Describe to Student B how and when you use it.

Student B: Listen to Student A's description. Ask follow-up questions and guess what the item is.

B Now change roles.

I can ask about uses.
☐ Very well ☐ I need more practice.

I can describe uses.
☐ Very well ☐ I need more practice.

See Language Booster page 69.

ONLINE PRACTICE

I think it's fun!

1 | Vocabulary

A Circle the correct word in each pair of sentences.

1. That movie was so *bored/ boring*. Was I the only one *bored/ boring* by it?

2. The teacher's explanation was *confused/ confusing*. I'm so *confused/ confusing*.

3. Don't get too *excited/ exciting*. You haven't seen the most *excited/ exciting* part yet.

4. I'm *interested/ interesting* in working for that company. They do *interested/ interesting* work.

5. We got *frustrated/ frustrating* waiting. It was a *frustrated/ frustrating* wait.

 B **PAIR WORK** Tell your partner about your experiences and how you felt. Use the words above.

2 | Conversation

CD2 **32** **A** Listen. What does Sonya think of the movie? What does Angela like about it?

Let's pause the movie and get a snack. Isn't the movie exciting, Sonya?

Not really. I think it's boring. **I feel like the acting isn't very good.**

Really?

Yeah, and to me, the story is kind of confusing.

I like it actually. In my opinion, the story is excellent.

If you ask me, the acting could be better.

Then why don't we watch something else? **I can finish this movie later.**

No, no, that's fine. I do want to see how it ends.

 B **PAIR WORK** Practice the conversation. Then exchange the blue and green words above with the words below and practice it again.

Sonya: **I find the acting terrible.** ▷ Angela: **I'm really enjoying it.**

Sonya: **Also, the story is confusing!** ▷ Angela: **I'll watch the rest another time.**

3 | Language Booster

A Notice the different ways we ask for and give opinions.

Asking for opinions	Giving opinions
What do you think of / How do you like the movie?	I think the movie is kind of boring. I feel like the acting isn't very good. I find the acting terrible. To me, the story is confusing. In my opinion, the acting is excellent. If you ask me, the acting could be better.

B **PAIR WORK** Think of three popular movies. Take turns asking for and giving opinions. Use the words in the Vocabulary section and your own ideas.

4 | Listening

 A Listen. Maria and Jason are discussing three different topics. Write each topic in the first column of the chart.

Topic	Maria's opinion	Jason's opinion

CD2 33 **B** Listen again. What are their opinions? Complete the rest of the chart.

ONLINE PRACTICE

SPEAK *with* CONFIDENCE

A **GROUP WORK** Discuss three of these topics, or think of other topics you want to discuss. Take turns asking for and giving opinions.

- an interesting company to work for
- the best smartphone apps
- an exciting movie you recently watched
- the most important language to study
- the best city to visit
- a frustrating traveling experience

B **GROUP WORK** Whose opinions are most similar to your own?

30 I feel the same way.

- **Agreeing with opinions**

- **Disagreeing with opinions**

1 | Vocabulary

A These words describe actions we can do. Write the correct word to make complete sentences.

apologize	argue	communicate	lie	forgive	gossip	judge

1. It's bad to _____ about other people when they aren't around.

2. It is OK to sometimes not tell the truth and _____.

3. People should _____ each other or they will be angry for a long time.

4. It's not OK for people to _____ in public.

5. People should _____ and express themselves properly.

6. If a person is wrong, they should _____.

7. I think it's not OK to _____ people by their looks.

 B **PAIR WORK** Underline the opinions you agree with. Rewrite any opinions you disagree with. Then compare and discuss with a partner.

Example:

A: In my opinion, gossiping about people behind their backs is mean.

B: I think so, too. I feel like it's immature.

2 | Conversation

CD2 **34** **A** Listen. Who are Joey and Mike? How does Caitlin feel about what happened?

Zack: Hi, Caitlin. It's Zack. Listen, I don't mean to gossip, but did you hear that Joey and Mike got into an argument?

Caitlin: I just heard. Our two best friends...

Zack: I don't really know what happened. To me, they just stopped communicating.

Caitlin: I think so, too. But I feel it's probably more than that. I think Mike sometimes argued with Joey and that bothered him.

Zack: I'm not sure I really agree. I've seen Joey judging Mike.

Caitlin: I just hope they make up or at least stay friends.

Zack: I feel the same way. Let's be sure to be there for them.

 B **PAIR WORK** Practice the conversation.

CD2 **35** **C** Listen. Write the two extra sentences you hear in the conversation. Practice the new conversation.

3|Language Booster

A Notice the different ways we agree and disagree with opinions.

Agreeing with opinions	Disagreeing with opinions
I agree.	I don't really agree.
I think so, too.	I'm not sure about that.
I completely agree with you.	I'm not sure I really agree.
I feel exactly the same way.	I don't feel that way at all.

B PAIR WORK Takes turns giving your opinion, and agreeing or disagreeing. Use the ideas below.

It's sometimes/never OK to…

tell a lie.   argue with your parents.

gossip about a friend.   judge people by their looks.

4|Pronunciation Stress in contrastive responses

CD2 **36** **A** Listen and practice. Notice how we stress a word that contrasts an idea.

A: In my opinion, it's never OK to lie.

B: I don't really agree. It's **sometimes** OK.

CD2 **37** **B** Listen. Underline the stressed word in each response. Listen and check your answers.
Then practice with a partner.

A: Are Brian and Cal gossiping?

B: No, they're arguing.

B: I think Brian should apologize.

A: You do? I feel Cal should apologize.

ONLINE PRACTICE

SPEAK *with* CONFIDENCE

A Think about what these proverbs mean to you.

Money doesn't grow on trees.

Never judge a book by its cover.

Love is blind.

Beauty is only skin deep.

Money can't buy happiness.

B GROUP WORK Discuss each proverb and share your opinions.

What do you think *"Money doesn't grow on trees"* means?

I think it means you shouldn't spend too much money.

31 What would you do?

- **Asking about an imaginary situation**
- **Discussing an imaginary situation**

1 | Vocabulary

A How would you feel if the things below happened to you? Write the correct letter next to each situation. More than one answer is possible.

| a. annoyed   b. embarrassed   c. nervous   d. concerned   e. thrilled   f. upset   g. puzzled   h. worried |

_____ 1. Someone forgot your birthday.

_____ 2. You forgot a friend's birthday.

_____ 3. A store clerk returned too much change.

_____ 4. A friend stopped calling you.

_____ 5. You won the lottery.

_____ 6. Your best friend is sick.

_____ 7. You lost your wallet.

_____ 8. You have a really important test the next day.

 B **PAIR WORK** Tell your partner how you would feel in the different situations above.

2 | Conversation

CD2 **38** **A** Listen. Why didn't Kevin go to Sandra's party? What does Amy think he should do?

Kevin: I am so embarrassed.

Amy: Why? **What happened?**

Kevin: I thought Sandra's birthday was on Sunday night. But it was on Saturday night.

Amy: Oh, no. So, you missed it?

Kevin: **What do you think I should do?**

Amy: I'd just be honest. **And definitely apologize.** I'd make sure to get her a birthday present, too!

Kevin: What time does the mall close?

 B **PAIR WORK** Practice the conversation. Then exchange the blue and green words above with the words below and practice it again.

Amy: **What did you do?**   Kevin: **What would you do?**   Amy: **And definitely say you're sorry.**

pair with VOCABULARY WORKSHEET 31

3 | Language Booster

A Notice the different ways we ask about and discuss an imaginary situation.

Asking about an imaginary situation	Discussing an imaginary situation
What would you do?	I would be honest.
What would you do if you were me?	I would definitely apologize.
What do you think I should do?	If I were you, I'd get her a birthday present.
How would you feel?	I'd probably feel embarrassed.

 B **PAIR WORK** Discuss the imaginary situations below. What do you think? How would you feel?

You lost your mobile phone.   A friend broke your laptop.   You got your dream job.

Examples:

A: I lost my mobile phone. What would you do if you were me?

B: I'd be really upset. I'd keep looking for it.

4 | Listening

A Listen to people describing things that happened to them. Circle how you think each person felt.

1. upset / thrilled / puzzled

2. embarrassed / confused / pleased

3. grateful / nervous / upset

4. annoyed / embarrassed / worried

B Listen again. Mark the statements T (true) or F (false).

1. _____ He didn't know anyone there.   3. _____ Her friend will probably be pleased.

2. _____ She doesn't know her neighbors.   4. _____ His friend was annoyed with him.

ONLINE PRACTICE

SPEAK *with* CONFIDENCE

 A **GROUP WORK** Discuss what you would do in these situations.

Someone gave you an expensive gift, but you don't like it.

A friend borrowed $100 and keeps forgetting to return it.

You found an envelope on the sidewalk with a large amount of money in it.

 B **GROUP WORK** Take turns completing the question "*What would you do if…?*" with your own ideas. Discuss what you would do in each situation.

32 Then what happened?

1 | Vocabulary

A Look at the words that describe qualities and values. Rank them from 1 (most important) to 8 (least important).

_____ generous _____ honest _____ loyal _____ ambitious

_____ competitive _____ sincere _____ modest _____ motivated

 B **PAIR WORK** Give your partner an example for the qualities above.

Examples:

A: My brother is competitive. He has to win even in friendly sports games.

B: My best friend is honest. She always tells the truth.

2 | Conversation

CD2 **40** **A** Listen. Where did the woman's money come from? What did she do with it?

Walt: I heard something interesting on the news last night before I went to bed.

Tara: Oh, yeah? What's that?

Walt: It was a story about a woman who gave away several million dollars. It was money she inherited from an aunt.

Tara: Wow! What did she do with it?

Walt: She was watching a TV show about needy families. After watching the show, she decided to give all the money away.

Tara: Amazing.

Walt: Next, she set up a scholarship program to pay for the education of hundreds of motivated high school kids. Then she decided to pay for their college tuition, too.

Tara: That's fantastic. She must be *really* generous!

 B **PAIR WORK** Practice the conversation.

CD2 **41** **C** Listen. Write the two extra sentences you hear in the conversation. Practice the new conversation.

3 | Language Booster

A Notice the different ways we describe a series of events.

> **Describing a series of events**
>
> **Before** I went to bed, I heard something interesting on the news.
>
> She was watching TV **when** she learned about some needy families.
>
> **After** watching the show, she decided to give all the money away.
>
> **Next,** she set up a scholarship program to pay for the education of high school kids.
>
> **Then** she decided to pay for their college tuition, too.

 B **PAIR WORK** Take turns adding follow-up sentences to the event below.

> A woman heard her neighbors lost their home in a fire.

Example:

A: A woman heard her neighbors lost their home in a fire.

B: Then she decided to help her neighbors.

A: Next, she…

4 | Pronunciation Intonation in clauses

 CD2 **42** **A** Listen and practice. Notice how each clause ends with falling intonation.

1. Before I went to bed, I heard something interesting on the news.

2. After she saw that, she decided to give all the money away.

B **PAIR WORK** Take turns completing these sentences. Pay attention to intonation.

1. After I woke up this morning, _____.

2. Before I came to class today, _____.

3. As soon as I got home last night, I _____.

ONLINE PRACTICE

SPEAK *with* CONFIDENCE

A Choose a word from the Vocabulary section.
Prepare a story that describes the quality.

 B **PAIR WORK** Share your stories. Others
ask follow-up questions.

A woman found a lost dog.

So, what did she do?

She brought the dog home. Then, she went to the police.

Is that the end of the story?

Not at all. She got a reward for finding the dog!

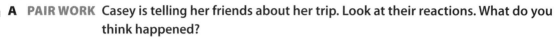

English in Action

ONLINE PRACTICE

OPINIONS

29

30

31

32

VIDEO

1 | Preview

A PAIR WORK Casey is telling her friends about her trip. Look at their reactions. What do you think happened?

B PAIR WORK You find a wallet with money but no ID in it. Check (✓) what you would do. Compare your answer with your partner.

_____ 1. I'd try to ask people on the street if it was theirs. Someone might be looking for it.

_____ 2. I would keep it. There is no ID and there's no way to find the person.

_____ 3. I'd bring it to the police. Someone might ask about it at the police station.

_____ 4. I'd give it to charity. It's not my money.

2 | Practice

A PAIR WORK Watch the video. What did Casey find? What happened as a result?

B Watch the video again. Who says these things? Casey, Eric, Tom, Jill or Maria? Write their names.

1. _____: "I complained, but they wouldn't give me my money back."

2. _____: "If I were you, I'd give it to the police."

3. _____: "You could stay at a nicer hotel!"

4. _____: "I don't know what I'd do."

5. _____: "I would be honest and give it to the police."

3 | Discuss

GROUP WORK Answer the questions.

1. What would you do if you didn't like your hotel room?

2. Do you video chat? With whom? What do you usually talk about?

CONFIDENCE BOOSTER

Student A: Turn to page 89.
Student B: Turn to page 97.

80

29 I think it's fun!

Student A and **Student B**: Take turns asking for and giving your opinions on these topics.

> the best place to visit in your country
>
> the worst household chore

I can ask for opinions.
☐ Very well   ☐ I need more practice.

I can give opinions.
☐ Very well   ☐ I need more practice.

See Language Booster page 73.

30 I feel the same way.

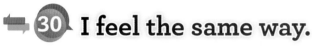

A Student A: Give your opinion about one of these topics.
Find out if Student B agrees or disagrees with you.

> borrowing money from friends   refunding a gift

Student B: Listen to Student A and give your own opinion.

B Now change roles.

I can agree with opinions.
☐ Very well   ☐ I need more practice.

I can disagree with opinions.
☐ Very well   ☐ I need more practice.

See Language Booster page 75.

31 What would you do?

Student A and **Student B**: Ask and answer questions about what you would do in these situations.

> A friend broke your camera.   You lost your homework.
>
> You won a free trip to go anywhere you want.

I can ask about imaginary situations.
☐ Very well   ☐ I need more practice.

I can discuss imaginary situations.
☐ Very well   ☐ I need more practice.

See Language Booster page 77.

32 Then what happened?

A Student A: Tell Student B about a situation where somebody behaved very honestly, generously, or sincerely.
Include as much information as you can.

Student B: Listen to what happened and ask follow-up questions.

B Now change roles.

I can describe a series of events.
☐ Very well   ☐ I need more practice.

See Language Booster page 79.

ONLINE PRACTICE

Student A
What does he look like?

1. Choose a person. Student B asks questions to guess the person you chose. Switch roles. Choose three more people each.

Example:

A: Is the person a man or a woman?

B: He's a man.

A: What does he look like?

B: He's bald.

Conversation Practice

2. Have a conversation with Student B by correctly completing (1–6). Read the first sentence to him or her. Listen to Student B's response (2). If it is correct, choose the next correct response to continue the conversation.

1. How's it going?

3. a. I'm looking for the teacher.
   b. Busy. I have a lot of homework. I also have a blog.

5. a. It's about technology trends. For example, did you know that most people in the world own a mobile phone?
   b. Most people own phones. People use their phones to send e-mails, watch videos, play games, and more!

Student A
How do you make sushi?

1a. Look at the steps to a recipe below. Place the steps in order. Use the words *first, then, next, after that,* and *Finally.*

Hummus

_____, blend again for 3–5 minutes or until smooth.

_____ chop in the blender for 1–2 minutes.

_____, pour canned chickpeas with ¼ of liquid from the can into a blender.

_____, serve with a flat bread.

_____, add lemon juice, tahini, garlic, and olive oil to the chopped chickpeas.

1b. Say your recipe above in the order you think is correct to Student B. He or she will correct you. Then listen to Student B's recipe below. Correct any mistakes you hear.

Sushi rolls

First, place seaweed on a bamboo roller. The rough side should be face-up.

Then add a layer of cooked rice to the seaweed.

Next, place raw fish and vegetables, or other ingredients you choose, on ¼ of the rice, near one end.

After that, use the roller to roll the seaweed.

Finally, cut into even pieces and serve.

Conversation Practice

2. Have a conversation with Student B (1–6). Read the first sentence to him or her. Listen to Student B's response (2). If it is correct, choose the next correct response to continue the conversation.

1. Good evening. May I take your order?

3. a. The service is great and it's not too expensive.
   b. The pad thai is very good and not very spicy.

5. a. What would you like to drink?
   b. Rice. Would you like white or brown?

Student A
What do you suggest?

1a. Look at the problems/desires below. Write suggestions or advice.

Problems/Desires	Suggestion/Advice
I have a cold.	
I have a sore back.	
I want to learn how to dance salsa.	
I need a new job.	

1b. Read the problems/desires below to Student B. Write his or her suggestions.

Problems/Desires	Suggestion/Advice
I need to lose weight.	
I really want to learn German.	
My head hurts.	
I can't sleep.	

Conversation Practice

2. Have a conversation with Student B (1–6). Read the first sentence to him or her. Listen to Student B's response (2). If it is correct, choose the next correct response to continue the conversation.

1. I need to lose weight.

3. a. I'd like to learn something new.
   b. What do you suggest I do?

5. a. Karate? I think dancing is easier than karate.
   b. Try not to eat at night.

Student A
Can you do the job?

1a. Look at the job posting below. Ask Student B questions to fill in the blanks.

Example:

A: Do you need experience?

B: No, you don't. Do you have to stand all day?

A: Yes, you do.

Job: Receptionist International Hotel

Description:

Work with a wide variety of international customers. Meet new people! Assist customers and greet them. Help customers check in and answer questions on the phone and in person.

Requirements:

_____ experience.

Should speak a second language.

_____ stand all day.

Must know the city.

_____ be cheerful.

Do not need college degree.

_____ a car.

1b. Share the pros and cons of the job with Student B. Make a list together.

Pros	Cons

Conversation Practice

2. Have a conversation with Student B (1–6). Read the first sentence to him or her. Listen to Student B's response (2). If it is correct, choose the next correct response to continue the conversation.

1. Hello, Princetown Services. How may I help you?

3. a. This is Mr. Kim speaking.
   b. You'd work weekends. Is that all right?

5. a. Hello, Mr. Riser. Mostly preparing briefs.
   b. Hello, Joe. I'm sorry, but the position was filled yesterday.

Student A
Why is Jon late?

1. Look at the charts below. Ask Student B questions to fill in the information.

   Example:

   A: What does Julia like to do in her free time?

   B: She likes to read a magazine and watch TV. Why is Jon late?

   A: He ran into a friend.

Name:	Julia
Free time:	
Wants to:	go to the beach
This weekend:	see a movie with a cousin, do laundry
Late because:	

Name:	Jon
Free time:	karaoke, listen to music
Wants to:	
This weekend:	
Late because:	ran into a friend

Conversation Practice

2. Have a conversation with Student B (1–6). Read the first sentence to him or her. Listen to Student B's response (2). If it is correct, choose the next correct response to continue the conversation.

   1. Would you like to see a movie tonight?

   3. a. Can you do your homework tonight and go to the movie tomorrow?
      b. Let's go to a movie tonight.

   5. a. Sure. Can you call me tomorrow morning?
      b. Sorry to hear it.

Student A
What time is the flight?

1. Look at the itinerary below. Ask Student B questions to fill in the information.

Example:

A: What time is the flight from San Francisco?

B: It leaves at 12:59 p.m. Where does the plane arrive?

A: It arrives in Heathrow Airport.

Travel Itinerary

Friday, June 6
OUP Airlines Flight#: 0930
Depart: San Francisco, __*12:59 p.m.*__ — SFO International
Arrive: London, June 7, 7:10 a.m. — Heathrow Airport

Saturday, June 7
Rail from London to Paris
Depart: London, 10 a.m. — St. Pancras Station
Arrive: Paris, 1:17 p.m. — _____

Hotel in Paris   Arrive: _____
Relais-Hotel du Vieux, Paris   Depart: June 10, 12 p.m.

Monday, June 10
Rail from Paris to _____
Depart: 6:59 p.m., Paris — Bercy Station
Arrive: _____ June 11, 7:16 a.m., — _____

Tuesday, June 11
Hotel in Milan   Arrive: _____
Via Scarlatti   Depart: June 14, 5 a.m.

Friday, June 14
HY Airlines Flight #: 1147
Depart: _____ June 14, 6:45 a.m. — _____
Arrive: Paris, June 14, 8:05 a.m. — Charles de Gaulle Airport
Depart: Paris, June 14, _____ — Charles de Gaulle Airport
Arrive: San Francisco, June 15, 12:05 a.m. — SFO International

---

Conversation Practice

2. Have a conversation with Student B (1–6). Read the first sentence to him or her. Listen to Student B's response (2). If it is correct, choose the next correct response to continue the conversation.

1. Where did you go for vacation? Did you go anywhere special?

3. a. Do you usually travel overseas or in your home country?
   b. You can't go overseas without a passport.

5. a. You're not permitted to take three bags.
   b. Do you need a visa to go to France?

Student A
It's normally used to fix things.

1. Look at the items below and choose one. Take turns telling Student B about your item. Be honest, but try to make it difficult for him or her to guess which item it is. Try to guess Student B's item before he or she guesses yours.

Example:

A: It's normally used to hold things.

B: Is it a backpack?

A: No, it isn't.

B: People generally use it to hold books.

A: Is it the shelf?

Swiss army knife	SUV	chair	swing	screwdriver
measuring cup	trash can	backpack	baby sling	baby stroller
tape	string	scissors	shelf	bag

Conversation Practice

2. Have a conversation with Student B (1–6). Read the first sentence to him or her. Listen to Student B's response (2). If it is correct, choose the next correct response to continue the conversation.

1. Could you do me a favor?

3. a. They drink a special beverage in Argentina called Mate.
   b. Could you buy me some Mate while you are in Argentina?

5. a. The most common feature is that it is served in a gourd.
   b. It's a hot drink people usually drink with friends.

Student A
What do you think?

1a. Look at the chart below. Ask and answer questions to find Katherine's opinion.

Example:

A: What does Katherine think about pizza?

B: She feels it's unhealthy. How does she like live theater?

A: She thinks it's boring.

	Katherine's opinion	Your partner's opinion
pizza		
smoking	awful	
eating at home		
live theater	boring	
cheese		
meeting new people	fascinating	
learning another language		
watching soaps on TV	exciting	
working in an office		
shopping for clothes	challenging	

1b. What do you and your partner think? Ask him or her if he or she agrees with Katherine's opinions. Write Student B's answers.

Example:

A: Katherine thinks pizza is unhealthy.

B: I'm not sure about that. It has cheese and tomatoes. I think it's healthy.

A: I disagree. It also has a lot of salt. I think Katherine is right. It's unhealthy.

Conversation Practice

2. Have a conversation with Student B (1–6). Read the first sentence to him or her. Listen to Student B's response (2). If it is correct, choose the next correct response to continue the conversation.

1. What did you think of the book?

3. a. I thought so, too. It's a beautiful story.
   b. I would be honest. It's very good.

5. a. I'd probably forgive and move on.
   b. I disagree. I wouldn't tell anyone.

What does he look like?

1. Choose a person. Student A asks questions to guess the person you chose. Switch roles. Choose three more people each.

Example:

A: Is the person a man or a woman?

B: He's a man.

A: What does he look like?

B: He's bald.

Conversation Practice

2. Have a conversation with Student A by completing (1–6). Listen to his or her sentence. Read the sentences in (2) and choose the correct response. Listen to Student A's response (3). If it is correct, choose the next correct response to continue the conversation.

2. a. Pretty good. And you?
   b. I'm going to the library. What are you doing?

4. a. A lot of my friends have blogs. What's yours about?
   b. What are you like?

6. I can't leave home without mine!

Student B
How do you make sushi?

1a. Look at the steps to a recipe below. Place the steps in order. Use the words *first, then, next, after that,* and *Finally*.

Sushi rolls

_____, place raw fish and vegetables, or other ingredients you choose, on ¼ of the rice, near one end.

_____, cut into even pieces and serve.

_____ add a layer of cooked rice to the seaweed.

_____, place seaweed on a bamboo roller. The rough side should be face-up.

_____, use the roller to roll the seaweed.

1b. Listen to Student A read the steps in the recipe below. Correct any mistakes you hear. Then say your recipe above in the order you think is correct to Student A. He or she will correct you.

Hummus

First, pour canned chickpeas with ¼ of liquid from the can into a blender.

Then chop in the blender for 1–2 minutes.

Next, add lemon juice, tahini, garlic, and olive oil to the chopped chickpeas.

After that, blend again for 3–5 minutes or until smooth.

Finally, serve with a flat bread.

Conversation Practice

2. Have a conversation with Student A by completing (1–6). Listen to his or her sentence. Read the sentences in (2) and choose the correct response. Listen to Student A's response (3). If it is correct, choose the next correct response to continue the conversation.

2. a. I've never had Thai food before. What do you recommend?
   b. Have you ever been to a Thai restaurant before?

4. a. I'll have an iced tea, please.
   b. That sounds good. What does it come with?

6. Brown, please. It's healthier.

Student B
What do you suggest?

1a. Look at the problems/desires below. Write suggestions or advice.

Problem/Desires	Suggestion/Advice
I need to lose weight.	
I really want to learn German.	
My head hurts.	
I can't sleep.	

1b. Read the problem/desires below to Student A. Write his or her suggestions.

Problem/Desires	Suggestion/Advice
I have a cold.	
I have a sore back.	
I want to learn how to dance salsa.	
I need a new job.	

Conversation Practice

2. Have a conversation with Student A by completing (1–6). Listen to his or her sentence. Read the sentences in (2) and choose the correct response. Listen to Student A's response (3). If it is correct, choose the next correct response to continue the conversation.

2 a. Why don't you exercise more?

  b. It's a good idea for people to exercise more.

4. a. I think you should learn karate.

  b. Are you getting enough sleep?

6. Then I think you should dance!

Student B
Can you do the job?

1a. Look at the job posting below. Ask Student A questions to fill in the blanks.

Example:

A: Do you need experience?

B: No, you don't. Do you have to stand all day?

A: Yes, you do.

Job: Receptionist International Hotel

Description:

Work with a variety of international clientele. Meet new people! Assist customers and greet them. Help customers check in and answer questions on the phone and in person.

Requirements:

Do not need experience.

_____ speak a second language.

Must be able to stand all day.

_____ know the city.

Must be cheerful.

_____ college degree.

Do not need a car.

1b. Share the pros and cons of the job with Student A. Make a list together.

Pros	Cons

Conversation Practice

2. Have a conversation with Student A by completing (1–6). Listen to his or her sentence. Read the sentences in (2) and choose the correct response. Listen to Student A's response (3). If it is correct, choose the next correct response to continue the conversation.

2. a. Hi. This is Joe. I need a job.

   b. Good morning. May I speak to Mr. Kim, please?

4. a. Mr. Kim, this is Joe Riser. Is the position of server still open?

   b. Hello, Mr. Kim. My name is Joe Riser. What are the hours?

6. Sorry to hear it. Thank you anyway.

Why is Jon late?

1. Look at people below. Ask Student A questions to fill in the information.

   Example:

   A: What does Julia like to do in her free time?

   B: She likes to read magazines and watch TV. Why is Jon late?

   A: He ran into a friend.

Name:	Julia
Free time:	read a magazine, watch TV
Wants to:	
This weekend:	
Late because:	The car wouldn't start.

Name:	Jon
Free time:	
Wants to:	go out to dinner
This weekend:	wash the car, do homework
Late because:	

Conversation Practice

2. Have a conversation with Student A by completing (1–6). Listen to his or her sentence. Read the sentences in (2) and choose the correct response. Listen to Student A's response (3). If it is correct, choose the next correct response to continue the conversation.

   2. a. Sorry, but I have to do my homework.
      b. I'd love to. Let's do homework together.

   4. a. Sorry, I'm late. The traffic was awful.
      b. That sounds good. Can I get back to you?

   6. a. Absolutely! That sounds good!

Student B
What time is the flight?

1. Look at the itinerary below. Ask Student A questions to fill in the information.

Example:

A: What time is the flight from San Francisco?

B: It leaves at 12:59 p.m. Where does the plane arrive?

A: It arrives in Heathrow Airport.

Travel Itinerary

Friday, June 6
OUP Airlines Flight#: 0930
Depart: San Francisco, 12:59 p.m. — _Heathrow Airport_
Arrive: London, June 7, 7:10 a.m. — _____

Saturday, June 7
Rail from London to Paris
Depart: London, _____ — St. Pancras Station
Arrive: Paris, 1:17 p.m. — Nord Station

Hotel in Paris   Arrive: June 7, 2 p.m.
Relais-Hotel du Vieux, Paris   Depart: _____

Monday, June 10
Rail from Paris to Florence
Depart: _____, Paris — _____
Arrive: Milan, June 11, 7:16 a.m. — Milano Centrale

Tuesday, June 11
Hotel in Milan   Arrive: June 11, 12 p.m.
Via Scarlatti   Depart: _____

Friday, June 14
HY Airlines Flight #: _____
Depart: Milan, June 14, _____ — Malpensa International
Arrive: Paris, June 14, 8:05 a.m. — Charles de Gaulle Airport
Depart: Paris, June 14, 9:45 a.m. — Charles de Gaulle Airport
Arrive: San Francisco, June 15, 12:05 a.m. — SFO International

---

Conversation Practice

2. Have a conversation with Student A by completing (1–6). Listen to his or her sentence. Read the sentences in (2) and choose the correct response. Listen to Student A's response (3). If it is correct, choose the next correct response to continue the conversation.

2. a. Yes, I went to Paris.
   b. Yes, I travelled with my family.

4. a. I usually prefer to visit other countries.
   b. I'd prefer to stay in a hotel.

6. Other Europeans don't need a visa, but I had to have one.

pair with **Student A** CONFIDENCE BOOSTER **21–24** *on p. 87*

It's normally used to fix things.

1. Look at the items below and choose one. Take turns telling Student A about your item. Be honest, but try to make it difficult for him or her to guess which item it is. Try to guess Student A's item before he or she guesses yours.

Example:

A: It's normally used to hold things.

B: Is it a backpack?

A: No, it isn't.

B: People generally use it to hold books.

A: Is it the shelf?

Swiss army knife	SUV	chair	swing	screwdriver
measuring cup	trash can	backpack	baby sling	baby stroller
tape	string	scissors	shelf	bag

Conversation Practice

2. Have a conversation with Student A by completing (1–6). Listen to his or her sentence. Read the sentences in (2) and choose the correct response. Listen to Student A's response (3). If it is correct, choose the next correct response to continue the conversation.

2. a. Sure. What do you need?
   b. Not at all.

4. a. Mate? What is it for?
   b. What do people usually drink in Argentina?

6. Sounds interesting. I'll look for it.

Student B
What do you think?

1a. Look at the chart below. Ask and answer questions to find Katherine's opinion.

Example:

A: What does Katherine think about pizza?

B: She feels it's unhealthy. How does she like live theater?

A: She thinks it's boring.

	Katherine's opinion	Your partner's opinion
pizza	unhealthy	
smoking		
eating at home	practical	
live theater		
cheese	delicious	
meeting new people		
learning another language	difficult	
watching soaps on TV		
working in an office	dull	
shopping for clothes		

1b. What do you and your partner think? Ask him or her if he or she agrees with Katherine's opinions. Write Student A's answers.

Example:

A: Katherine thinks pizza is unhealthy.

B: I'm not sure about that. It has cheese and tomatoes. I think it's healthy.

A: I disagree. It also has a lot of salt. I think Katherine is right. It's unhealthy.

Conversation Practice

2. Have a conversation with Student A by completing (1–6). Listen to his or her sentence. Read the sentences in (2) and choose the correct response. Listen to Student A's response (3). If it is correct, choose the next correct response to continue the conversation.

2. a. I thought the movie was kind of boring.
   b. To me, the story was wonderful.

4. a. What would you do if it happened to you?
   b. How would you feel if I liked the book?

6. I disagree. I'd want to get even.

Audio and Video Scripts

LESSON 1
Conversation, Part A
Nicole: Hi. How's it going? I'm Nicole.

Brian: Pretty good. My name's Brian.

Nicole: And where are you from?

Brian: I'm from Canada. And you?

Nicole: Brazil.

Brian: I went to Brazil last year!

Nicole: Really? Wow. Did you travel alone?

Brian: No, I went with friends. It was fun. Listen, I'd better get going.

Conversation, Part C
Nicole: Hi. How's it going? I'm Nicole.

Brian: Pretty good. My name's Brian.

Nicole: And where are you from?

Brian: I'm from Canada. And you?

Nicole: Brazil. Have you been there?

Brian: I went to Brazil last year!

Nicole: Really? Wow. Did you travel alone?

Brian: No, I went with friends. It was fun. Listen, I'd better get going. I don't want to be late.

LESSON 2
Conversation, Part A
Nathan: Excuse me. I'm looking for my wife.

Clerk: What does she look like?

Nathan: Well, she's tall and thin.

Clerk: Does she have red hair?

Nathan: No. My wife has dark brown hair.

Clerk: What's she wearing?

Nathan: A blue skirt and a white blouse.

Clerk: Is that her by the changing room?

Nathan: Yes. I guess she wants that coat.

Listening, Part A and B
A: Great party, isn't it?

B: Yeah, but I don't know many people here.

A: You don't? Do you know Paula?

B: No.

A: Oh, well that's her over there. Do you see her? She has blond hair. And she's in her early thirties. She's wearing a black dress.

B: She looks nice.

A: She's talking to Reggie, her cousin.

B: Yeah. And where's Wally? I've heard of him, but I don't know him.

A: This party is for him. He's over there.

B: What does he look like?

A: He's short and a little heavy. He's wearing a green sweater.

B: How old is he?

A: He's twenty-two.

B: And who's that man by the food table?

A: The middle-aged one? That's Adam. He's Paula's older brother.

B: He's really thin. Oh, look! Valerie is here.

A: Who?

B: My friend Valerie. See her? She's really pretty. She has black hair and she's wearing a blue dress.

A: The one by the door?

B: Yeah. Do you want me to introduce you?

A: Sure!

LESSON 3
Conversation, Part A
Yasuko: Mary, your twin girls look so much alike. How do you tell them apart?

Mary: Actually, they have very different personalities.

Yasuko: Oh? In what way?

Mary: Matilda is very outgoing and talkative.

Yasuko: And what about her sister?

Mary: Alice is more serious. And she can be very impatient sometimes.

Yasuko: I see they both like to draw.

Mary: Yes, they're both very creative. They love to make things.

Listening, Part A and B
1. I have a new friend, Nora. We're the same in some ways, but different in other ways. Nora is very outgoing. She likes to be around people. I'm not really outgoing. I'm shy. But we're still good friends. She's also confident. In math class, she always shouts out the answers. She is sometimes right but sometimes wrong. She doesn't care. She just tries. I like that about her.

2. The new guy in our class, Simon, is interesting to me. He's really good at art. He's creative and loves anime. He wants to be an anime artist someday. But he's also very good at math. He's probably the best student in our class, actually. He gets good grades easily, but he hardly studies. He's becoming a good friend.

3. I work in a coffee shop on weekends and there's a new girl there. Her name's Caley. She's not hardworking at all and gets very impatient with customers. You know, sometimes customers need time to choose their order. Caley just looks the other way and taps her fingers like this. She also forgets the customers' orders and makes lots of mistakes. I don't think she'll have this job for very long.

LESSON 4
Conversation, Part A
Ellen: What are you doing?
Luke: I'm just sending an e-mail.
Ellen: Do you always use your phone to send e-mails? All of my friends text these days.
Luke: Some of my friends text, some don't. That e-mail was to my dad.
Ellen: So, what else do you use your phone for?
Luke: I often use it to play games. A lot of my friends watch movies, but I find the screen too small.
Ellen: Do you use it for social networking?
Luke: Sure, all the time. Say, I don't think we're friends online….

Conversation, Part C
Ellen: What are you doing? Are you busy?
Luke: I'm just sending an e-mail.
Ellen: Do you always use your phone to send e-mails? All of my friends text these days.
Luke: Some of my friends text, some don't. That e-mail was to my dad. He sends me e-mails every day.
Ellen: So, what else do you use your phone for?
Luke: I often use it to play games. A lot of my friends watch movies, but I find the screen too small.
Ellen: Do you use it for social networking?

Luke: Sure, all the time. Say, I don't think we're friends online…

LESSONS 1–4 ENGLISH IN ACTION
Maria: Eric, how can you study and text at the same time?
Eric: Most of my classmates text, study, and tweet at the same time these days.
Maria: Hi Tom! How's it going?
Tom: Good. How are you?
Maria: OK. Eric and I are studying. Well, actually I'm studying.
Eric: Hey! So am I.
Tom: Hi, Jill.
Jill: Oh. Hey Tom!
Tom: What are you doing?
Jill: Oh, I'm waiting for my cousin. She's on her way from the airport.
Tom: Your cousin?
Jill: Yeah, she's going to stay with Maria and me for a couple of months. Her name's Casey.
Tom: Really? Where's she from?
Eric: Los Angeles.
Tom: What's she like?
Jill: Oh, she's really fun. And…different. She's *really* different from me!
Tom: Different…in what way?
Eric: Everyone. Casey's in a taxi.
Tom: How do YOU know Casey?
Eric: We're Facebook friends. She just updated her status—I'm in a taxi, and heading to Jill's place!
Maria: How are you studying?
Eric: Trust me. I am.
Tom: OK. So, what's she like?
Jill: Oh yeah, uh, well. She's really into clothes. She likes to wear lots of accessories—things she makes herself. Hats, scarves, and stuff.
Tom: So how old is she?
Jill: She's…let me remember…she's—
Eric: 21.
Jill: Right. 21. Oh! I just got a text. Casey is—
Eric: Here!
Maria: Wow.

Eric: I know!

Jill: I'm going to get her.

Maria: OK…done! I'm finished with my homework.

Eric: I haven't even started.

Maria: See. I told you. Not many of us can do two things at the same time.

Jill: Everyone. This is Casey!

Casey: Hi!

Tom/Eric/Maria: Hi Casey!!

Casey: Nice to meet you. It's cold here!

Tom: Let's go get something warm to drink.

Maria: Coffee sounds good!

Jill: Eric?

Eric: I can't. I have to do homework. But will you guys text me what you're talking about?

Jill/Maria/Tom: No.

LESSON 5

Conversation, Part A

Kent: Hi, Lori. I'm getting hungry.

Lori: Hey, Kent! Me too. Have you ever tried Mexican food? I know a great place.

Kent: No, I haven't. But I think I want Asian food.

Lori: OK. How about Thai?

Kent: I've never had Thai food.

Lori: It's my favorite! The noodle dishes are amazing!

Kent: Do you have a place in mind?

Lori: There's a place called *Thairiffic*.

Kent: OK. I'll meet you there!

Listening, Part A and B

1. I've had this several times. But it's not easy to get fresh. I've often had it as juice. The first time I tried it, I didn't know what to expect. It was very sour. I've only tried sweet fruit, but I really liked it. I would recommend this to anyone.

2. I love most types of seafood but this one? I'm not so sure. Well, I know it's popular, but I'm not sure why. I just remember it was expensive. And it looked dangerous. When I tasted it, I just remember thinking, "It's so salty." I like salty food but not this. Oh, and it's raw. Have you ever had it?

3. I tried this once in the United States. It's popular in the south. It's a vegetable that not a lot of people know, or like. It's in dishes like gumbo, and I hear that it is delicious. I've never tried gumbo. I just had this vegetable fried. It was really bland. I didn't like the texture at all.

4. This is one of my favorite foods. I tried it the first time when I was eight-years-old. I remember the taste was really strong. But I guess I like strong flavors because I eat this all the time. I like it in salads, on crackers, and with fruit.

LESSON 6

Conversation, Part A

Joel: What are you making?

Tara: Bruschetta. Have you ever tried it?

Joel: No. How do you make it?

Tara: First, grill the bread. Make sure you grill both sides. Then rub the bread with garlic.

Joel: OK. It smells good.

Tara: Next, pour olive oil on the bread. Don't pour too much, just a little. After that, put on some chopped tomatoes. Finally, add salt, pepper, and a basil leaf. Try one!

Conversation, Part C

Joel: What are you making?

Tara: Bruschetta. Have you ever tried it?

Joel: No. How do you make it?

Tara: First, grill the bread. Make sure you grill both sides. Then rub the bread with garlic. Do this right away.

Joel: OK. It smells good. What do I do next?

Tara: Next, pour olive oil on the bread. Don't pour too much, just a little. After that, put on some chopped tomatoes. Finally, add salt, pepper, and a basil leaf. Try one! You'll love it!

LESSON 7

Conversation, Part A

Kit: So, what are you in the mood for?

Sarah: Have you tried that new restaurant near the subway station?

Kit: You mean *The Pink Peppercorn?*

Sarah: Yeah. That's the one.

Kit: No, I haven't yet. What's it like?

Sarah: It's pretty good. They serve a lot of curries and noodle dishes. And their prices are reasonable. Most of the dishes cost about $10.

Kit: That's pretty good. What's the service like?

Sarah: The service is really slow, but otherwise it's a nice place.

Kit: I think I'll try it!

Listening, Part A and B

1. A: They've done a nice job with the decoration.

   B: I like the colors.

   A: So do I. And the music is good. It's not too loud.

   B: I hate restaurants with loud, noisy music. You can't hear yourself think!

   A: I know. This place feels really relaxed.

2. A: But it's too bad it's so far.

   B: Yeah. It's not near anything.

   A: I heard it's hard to get space downtown.

   B: I don't think many customers will come here.

   A: I agree. It takes too long to get here.

3. A: The menu looks really good.

   B: Where do we start? Some of the chicken dishes look nice.

   A: They're famous for their seafood.

   B: Oh, yeah? I see they have octopus.

   A: I've never tried that. Oh, I can't decide!

4. A: But I think they need to hire more people.

   B: I agree. The servers are really busy. They need one or two more.

   A: And our server made a mistake with our meal. That's not good.

B: She didn't even know the menu very well.

A: Yeah—she couldn't answer many questions.

5. A: Wow! Our bill is only $29.

   B: That's very reasonable.

   A: A new restaurant can't charge too much.

   B: I know. Or they won't get much business.

   A: I hope they're making money at least.

LESSON 8

Conversation, Part A

Server: Welcome to Zippy's. Are you ready to order?

Customer: Yes, I'd like the fried chicken, please.

Server: Would you like mashed potatoes, French fries, or steamed rice with that?

Customer: Hm…I'll take steamed rice.

Server: Anything to drink?

Customer: I'll have the peach iced tea.

Server: Anything else? Would you like to start with an appetizer?

Customer: No, I'm saving room for dessert.

Conversation, Part C

Server: Welcome to Zippy's. Are you ready to order?

Customer: Yes, I'd like the fried chicken, please. I'm pretty hungry.

Server: Would you like mashed potatoes, French fries, or steamed rice with that?

Customer: Hm…I'll take steamed rice.

Server: Anything to drink?

Customer: I'll have the peach iced tea.

Server: Anything else? Would you like to start with an appetizer?

Customer: No, I'm saving room for dessert. I'll take a chocolate cake!

LESSONS 5–8 ENGLISH IN ACTION

Tom: What time are Casey, Jill, and Maria coming over for dinner?

Eric: 7. We have plenty of time. What should we make?

Tom: Pasta!

Eric: Tom, I love your pasta but—

Tom: I love it too. I could have it every single day.

Eric: Exactly my point. We do have it every day. We should try something different. Let me see…have you tried Indian food?

Tom: No, I haven't.

Eric: How about Japanese food?

Tom: Nope.

Eric: What have you tried?

Tom: Pasta.

Eric: OK. Nevermind…Casey likes fish. So do Jill and Maria. Let's make a simple fish dish.

Tom: OK.

Eric: OK. Fry the vegetables in a pan.

Eric: Don't forget to add salt…pepper…and olive oil.

Eric: Don't pour too much olive oil, just a little.

Eric: I have to get the phone.

Tom: Go ahead. Don't worry.

Eric: Thanks, Tom.

Tom: Oh, no! The fish!

Eric: What's wrong?

Tom: I'm sorry.

Eric: We still have time. It's not a big deal. We can just order in.

Tom: I know a great place we can order from! The food is pretty good, it's fairly cheap, and attracts a lot of customers.

Eric: OK. Sounds good.

Server: Hello?

Tom: Hello, can I place a delivery order?

Server: Sure! What would you like?

Tom: I would like your…hm…

Server: Tom?

Tom: Yes…Roberto?

Server: Yes! How are you?

Tom: Great!

Server: What can I get you? Is it the usual?

Tom: Yes, but for five people.

Server: Sure thing. Five of our special house pastas.

Tom: Sounds delicious! And can you put extra tomato sauce and cheese in one of them?

Server: Anything for you, Tom!

Tom: Thank you.

Server: Have a good night!

Tom: What?

Eric: Pasta?

Tom: You said something different. And it's not my pasta, so it's different…right?

LESSON 9
Conversation, Part A

Leila: Hi, Tracey. I'm not feeling too well.

Tracey: Oh? What's the matter, Leila?

Leila: I have a sore throat.

Tracey: That's too bad. I hope it's not the flu. Have you seen a doctor?

Leila: No. I'm fine, really. I think I just have a cold.

Tracey: You have a fever. Why don't you go home and rest?

Leila: Good idea. Can you take notes for me in class?

Tracey: Sure. I hope you feel better soon.

Leila: Thanks.

Listening, Part A and B

1. A: So, how was your weekend?

   B: It was so-so. Look what I did.

   A: That looks really painful. What happened?

   B: I was playing tennis and I fell.

   A: Oh, no! Does it hurt?

   B: Oh, yeah. Luckily, I didn't break it. I went to a doctor, she took an X-ray and just put a bandage on it. But it's really difficult to hold anything. I can't even write or type with it.

   A: I would think it's a good idea not to use it at all.

   B: I guess.

2. A: Did that medicine I gave you do you any good?

   B: Well, I feel a bit better today.

   A: That's good.

   B: But it hasn't completely gone away. I'm sure it was the fish I had at the restaurant. I don't think it was very fresh.

   A: Yeah, it was probably that. The chicken I had was fine.

   B: I don't think I want to go back there.

A: Try not to eat anything too oily or spicy for a few days. Just rice and soup would be good. And drink lots of water.

3. A: How do I look?

   B: Not too good. They're both really red, especially the left one.

   A: Still?

   B: I'm afraid so. Are they sore?

   A: Not at all. And I can still see perfectly fine.

   B: Why don't you get some medicine for it? You don't want it to get any worse.

   A: I suppose.

   B: Better yet, I suggest seeing a doctor. You can't be too careful.

   A: Do you think it was the contacts?

   B: Maybe. It's a good idea to wear your glasses for a while.

4. A: I need another aspirin. It's not going away. Actually, I think it's getting worse.

   B: That's not good. Why don't you put a cold cloth on your forehead?

   A: Good idea.

   B: And I'll turn off this light. The bright lights don't help.

   A: Thanks.

   B: Why don't you go and lie down in bed?

   A: OK.

   B: And I'll check on you in a little while.

LESSON 10

Conversation, Part A

Alex: I've been so tired lately. I never seem to have enough energy. Should I join a gym?

Luisa: Gyms can be expensive. There are simple ways to exercise at home.

Alex: Like what?

Luisa: If I were you, I'd climb the stairs or dance to music. You should do something active that you enjoy. Are you getting enough sleep?

Alex: Sure. I sleep about ten hours a day.

Luisa: That's too much. Getting too much sleep can make you feel tired. You should try to sleep eight hours a day.

Conversation, Part C

Alex: I've been so tired lately. I never seem to have enough energy. Should I join a gym?

Luisa: Gyms can be expensive. There are simple ways to exercise at home.

Alex: Like what? What would you do?

Luisa: If I were you, I'd climb the stairs or dance to music. You should do something active that you enjoy. Are you getting enough sleep?

Alex: Sure. I sleep about ten hours a day. But I'm still tired.

Luisa: That's too much. Getting too much sleep can make you feel tired. You should try to sleep eight hours a day.

LESSON 11

Conversation, Part A

Rachel: I really need to get more exercise.

Peter: Me too. We could take classes at the sports center. There's racquetball, boxing, swimming—

Rachel: Oh, I wouldn't really like those. They seem like a lot of hard work.

Peter: Well, how about a class in ballroom dancing? I'd love to try that!

Rachel: Really? Why is that?

Peter: Because I'd learn something new. And I can do it with someone else.

Rachel: I think it would be boring. I'd like to try something more relaxing, like tai chi.

Listening, Part A and B

1. I've always wanted to try this. This would be perfect for me because I love the water and like to be on my own a lot. I like it because you don't need too much equipment, just a boat and a paddle. I wouldn't want to go too far, at least until I build my upper body strength. And I'd like to try it on a lake, not in the ocean. It looks like a very peaceful activity, if you know what I mean.

2. I think this is a pretty common game, or I guess it's a sport, actually. My older brother plays a lot, but I've never tried it. I'm a very competitive person, and this looks like non-stop action. To be honest, I'd like to beat my

brother! It also just looks fun, so I hope to try it soon. My friend has a table at his house, so maybe he'll let me play sometime.

3. I've wanted to try this for a long time. It looks so relaxing, but I'm sure it's hard work, too. There's a sports center in town with an indoor swimming pool that offers classes three times a week. I don't think I'd want to go that often, but maybe once or twice a week. None of my friends do this, so it might be a good way to meet some new people. I'm not a very good swimmer, but I don't think that matters.

4. I would so love to do this. It goes back thousands of years, so there is an interesting tradition around it. Of course, in the past it was hunting, but that doesn't interest me. I'd do it just with regular targets. I remember I saw it on TV at the Olympics Games a couple of years ago and found it fascinating. It doesn't look easy at all. I'd like to try it because I want to get into something that requires discipline.

LESSON 12

Conversation, Part A

Celine: So, I just got this great new sports channel. All sports, all the time.

Doug: Cool. So, what should we watch?

Celine: Let's see…how about tennis?

Doug: Um, is it OK if we watch something different? Tennis is kind of boring to watch.

Celine: Sure. Golf is more interesting than tennis, don't you think?

Doug: Not really. I think golf is less interesting than tennis. I do like soccer. It's my favorite.

Celine: Mine too, but there are no soccer games today. Say, do you want to go for a walk?

Conversation, Part C

Celine: So, I just got this great new sports channel. All sports, all the time.

Doug: Cool. So, what should we watch?

Celine: Let's see…how about tennis? I love tennis.

Doug: Um, is it OK if we watch something different? Tennis is kind of boring to watch.

Celine: Sure. Golf is more interesting than tennis, don't you think?

Doug: Not really. I think golf is less interesting than tennis. I do like soccer. It's my favorite.

Celine: Mine too, but there are no soccer games today. Say, do you want to go for a walk? I can use the exercise.

LESSONS 9–12 ENGLISH IN ACTION

Eric: Help yourselves. Enjoy.

Casey/Jill: Thank you. Thanks, Eric!

Eric: Thank you!

Jill: So, how did your doctor's appointment go last week?

Eric: Oh, not so well, actually.

Casey: That's too bad. Nothing serious, I hope.

Eric: Oh, no, nothing like that. I can't sleep at night, and sometimes my stomach hurts.

Casey: Oh, no!

Eric: It's OK. My doctor said I should change my diet.

Jill: Change your diet?

Eric: Yeah, she said I should eat healthy. I think I eat pretty healthy.

Jill: Um…well, it's a not good idea to eat too much sugar.

Eric: No, of course not. The doctor said I should stop drinking coffee. But I love coffee. It's been real hard. He said I should also eat more vegetables.

Casey: I can't see you as a vegetarian somehow.

Eric: No, I don't have to give up meat, but I should eat more vegetables.

Jill: I think you should exercise more. I exercise three times a week and I feel healthy.

Eric: Exercise? I bowl four times a week.

Casey: Really? That's exercise.

Eric: Yeah! I guess it is.

Casey: Wow, you must be really good.

Eric: I beat all the other players! And I also box.

Jill: I didn't know that!

Eric: I box almost every day! I'm really good at it too. Boxing is definitely more fun than bowling.

Casey: Wow, you're really athletic!

Eric: Yep. And I also play tennis.

Casey/Jill: Tennis?

Eric: Yep. Tennis was more difficult to learn than boxing. But I win almost every game now. You guys want to see me play?

Jill: Like, right now?

Eric: Sure!

LESSON 13

Conversation, Part A

Josh: So, how's school going?

Lily: Well, I'm getting mostly A's and B's. But I'm not doing so well in Portuguese. I'm not very good at languages, I guess.

Josh: No one is good at every subject.

Lily: I suppose. So, are your classes going OK?

Josh: My accounting class is hard. I don't think I'm very good with numbers. But my literature teacher says I'm a good writer.

Lily: You'd make a great journalist.

Josh: As long as I don't write about numbers.

Conversation, Part C

Josh: So, how's school going? How are your grades?

Lily: Well, I'm getting mostly A's and B's. But I'm not doing so well in Portuguese. I'm not very good at languages, I guess.

Josh: No one is good at every subject. I wouldn't worry.

Lily: I suppose. So are your classes going OK?

Josh: My accounting class is hard. I don't think I'm very good with numbers. But my literature teacher says I'm a good writer.

Lily: You'd make a great journalist.

Josh: As long as I don't write about numbers.

LESSON 14

Conversation, Part A

Katy: I want to start my own business after I graduate.

Raul: Really?

Katy: I just need to have some money to get started. And I need to have a fresh idea.

Raul: Do you have any ideas?

Katy: I'd like to sell healthy lunches to people in offices, things like sandwiches and salads.

Raul: Do you think it would be difficult to get started?

Katy: Well, I would need a good kitchen. But I wouldn't have to have a car. I could use a bicycle.

Raul: Good idea.

Katy: Say, I'm looking for a business partner. Are you interested?

Listening, Part A and B

1. First, I want to thank your teacher, Mrs. Perez, for letting me talk to you today about being a model. Now, there are different types of models. For example, there are fashion models and print models. For any type of modeling, you need to have clear skin and healthy hair. You have to look healthy. But you don't have to be thin to be a successful model. If we only think of fashion modeling, yes, it's important. But there are many models that we consider *plus size* and these models are more typical of the average person. Finally, you don't have to have a college degree, but I encourage you all to get a degree. A model's career can be short, and you will want to have another set of skills to fall back on.

2. Hi, everyone. I am a concierge. I work at a hotel, and I help guests. I make travel arrangements, give advice on local restaurants, deliver messages—that kind of thing. So, if you're interested in a career as a concierge, what skills do you need to have? Well, you need to be friendly. No one wants to talk to an unfriendly concierge! Also, you have to know the area around the hotel or the city. A concierge often gives directions. You don't

usually have to work late at night. That's another thing I like about the job—the hours. We mostly work during the day. That's when our guests need us most. Finally, you will notice I am wearing a uniform. You have to wear a uniform of course, so if you don't want to wear a uniform at your job, this isn't the job for you.

3. Hello. From what I am wearing, can anyone guess what my job is? No? Well, I'm an architect. There are a lot of things that are necessary if you want to be an architect. We design buildings, so many people think we don't need to know about interior design. Not true—we do. And another thing we need to be good at is math. So, if you want to be an architect, keep taking those algebra and geometry classes. You also have to be able to work on a team. We work with all kinds of people. Some think architects spend all their time alone, and again this is not true. That's what I like about my job—working with others. Now, an architect needs a lot of education and yes, you need a license. It's necessary since architects have to design safe buildings for people to live and work in.

LESSON 15

Conversation, Part A

Ron: Hi, Keiko. Are you enjoying your new job?

Keiko: Yeah. So far so good. I get to meet lots of interesting people.

Ron: You're a concierge, right?

Keiko: Yes. I work for the new hotel downtown.

Ron: Do you get to use your language skills?

Keiko: I do. I use both my French and English.

Ron: And how's the salary?

Keiko: Well, I'm still in training, but I'll get a raise when I'm done.

Listening, Part A and B

1. I thought I wouldn't enjoy the job when I first started. I don't really like working at night. But I didn't have a choice since I'm one of the new guys. At first, I was worried about sitting down all day. And I don't know the city very well. Luckily, with GPS it's very easy to take people where they want to go. Most of my trips are short distances or to the airport. Some of the people I drive are really interesting.

2. I really like my job because I've always loved food. I'm learning a lot about how to make some really great dishes in the kitchen. And we get great food for free. That's the best thing. It can get really stressful at times. But the atmosphere is nice there, and I'm working with a great group of people.

3. It's kind of a fun job if you enjoy selling things. We have a great range of stuff in the store, and I love seeing all the latest designs when they come in. However, I wish I had a different boss. This guy is always bothering me to try to get people to buy things. I prefer to let customers take their time. No one wants to feel pressured, you know?

4. I've always enjoyed working in a place like this. It's really popular with kids. They love to come and look at what we have. They always want to pick them up and play with them, so it's kind of fun. Especially, the baby ones. I love playing with them, too. The only thing I don't like is that it takes me about two hours to get here. I really should move and live closer to my work.

LESSON 16

Conversation, Part A

Manager: Hello. Java Coffee.

Evan: Hello. Can I speak to the manager, please?

Manager: This is the manager.

Evan: Oh, good afternoon. My name is Evan Kincaid. I'm calling about the server position you advertised. Is it still available?

Manager: It is. We haven't filled it yet.

Evan: Great! Can I ask—what are the hours?

Manager: You'd work on weekends only. It's a part-time job.

Evan: That's perfect. And what would my responsibilities be?

Manager: Mostly serving coffee and some light cleaning.

Evan: OK. Do you require any previous experience?

Manager: Not at all. We provide all the training you need. Do you want to come in for an interview?

Evan: Yes! I can come in today!

Conversation, Part C

Manager: Hello. Java Coffee. This is Susana.

Evan: Hello. Can I speak to the manager, please?

Manager: This is the manager.

Evan: Oh, good afternoon. My name is Evan Kincaid. I'm calling about the server position you advertised. Is it still available?

Manager: It is. We haven't filled it yet.

Evan: Great! Can I ask—what are the hours? Also, which days is it?

Manager: You'd work on weekends only. It's a part-time job.

Evan: That's perfect. And what would my responsibilities be?

Manager: Mostly serving coffee and some light cleaning.

Evan: OK. Do you require any previous experience?

Manager: Not at all. We provide all the training you need. Do you want to come in for an interview?

Evan: Yes! I can come in today!

LESSONS 13–16 ENGLISH IN ACTION

Tom: Hi, guys. I heard you might be going to Australia, Casey!

Casey: Yep. I'm looking for a part-time job to save up. Maria is helping me.

Maria: This company is looking for a translator.

Casey: I don't speak any other languages.

Tom: I wouldn't recommend the job then. This coffee shop is looking for a server. Why not here?

Casey: I would have to deal with angry people. I also would have to work late at night. Then I couldn't enjoy my stay here.

Maria: And tips aren't steady.

Casey: Yes. That is true too.

Maria: What about this? A fashion company is looking for a part-time assistant.

Tom: And they need someone to start right away!

Casey: That sounds perfect!

Maria: You should call them.

Casey: OK.

Employee: Fashion INC.

Casey: Hi! Could I speak to the manager?

Employee: This is the manager.

Casey: My name is Casey. I was wondering if the part-time assistant position was still available.

Employee: Yes. We haven't filled it yet.

Casey: What sort of position is it?

Employee: You would be helping around the office.

Casey: What are the hours?

Employee: Four times a week from 9am to 2pm.

Casey: That's perfect.

Employee: Why don't you come in for an interview?

Casey: Great!

[later that day…]

Casey: Hello. I'm here for the interview for the part-time assistant position. Can I speak to the manager?

Employee: Yes. You can.

Casey: Great!

Employee: What's your name?

Casey: My name is Casey!

Employee: Oh, Casey. Yes.

Casey: It's great to meet you. I just want to tell you, I can write pretty well. I have a fashion blog. I'm also really good with people. And as you can see, I'm good at fashion.

Employee: Sounds good.

Casey: I'm also reliable and a hard worker. I can do a really good job.

Employee: Sounds like you'd be a great assistant.

Casey: Really? When can I start?

Employee: Oh, I don't know. You have to
interview first.

Casey: This isn't the interview?

Employee: No, let me call the manager… Hi,
Ben? This is Mike from downstairs.
Casey is here to see you…

LESSON 17

Conversation, Part A

A: So, how do you like it here so far, Steve?

B: It's great, Ann. I'm learning a lot.

A: Are you working tomorrow?

B: No, that's my day off.

A: Lucky you. What do you do in your free time?

B: I like to play sports.

A: Oh, yeah? That's interesting. What do
you play?

B: Soccer, basketball, baseball, hockey, tennis…

Listening, Part A and B

1. A: So, what do you like to do in your free
time, Paul?

B: Well, actually I love to cook.

A: Cooking? Really?

B: Yeah. I like it a lot.

A: So, what kinds of things do you like
to cook?

B: It depends. Usually, I just look for
interesting recipes on the Internet, and I try
them out.

A: Do you ever cook for your friends?

B: No, I just cook for myself.

A: Oh.

2. A: Do you have any hobbies, Anna?

B: Hobbies? Well not exactly, but I like music.
I play the guitar. I often play down at the
mall on weekends.

A: Really?

B: Yeah, I usually set up outside in front of
the entrance. I put a hat down in front of
me. People often leave me a dollar or two if
they like my music.

A: Cool. So, do you make much?

B: Well, on a good day I can make
around $50.

3. A: How do you spend your free time, Tim?

B: Oh, I'm really into photography. I love it.

A: Oh, yeah? What sort of things do you
photograph?

B: Mainly wildlife. I like to take photos
of birds and animals, you know,
nature pictures.

A: That's interesting.

B: I'm going to have a show at the public
library next month.

A: That's great! Make sure you let me know
when. I'd love to see it.

LESSON 18

Conversation, Part A

Jeff: Hey Kirk, do you have plans for
Friday night?

Kirk: Friday night? I don't think so. Why?

Jeff: Do you want to see a movie?

Kirk: Sure, I'd love to. What's playing?

Jeff: *Free Fall* is playing at the theater.

Kirk: Great! I love action movies. When do
you want to meet?

Jeff: How about at 7 p.m., in front of
the theater?

Kirk: OK. And let's get some pizza after
the movie.

Jeff: Sounds good. See you then!

Conversation, Part C

Jeff: Hey Kirk, do you have plans for
Friday night?

Kirk: Friday night? I don't think so. Why?

Jeff: Do you want to see a movie?

Kirk: Sure, I'd love to. What's playing?

Jeff: *Free Fall* is playing at the theater. I heard
it's good.

Kirk: Great! I love action movies. When do
you want to meet?

Jeff: How about at 7 p.m., in front of
the theater?

Kirk: OK. And let's get some pizza after the
movie. I know a great place.

Jeff: Sounds good. See you then!

LESSON 19

Conversation, Part A

Beth: Hello?

Chen: Beth? Hi, it's Chen.

Beth: Hi! How's everything?

Chen: Great. Listen, would you like to go to the museum later?

Beth: I'm sorry, but I can't.

Chen: Really? Why not?

Beth: I have to go to work. Do you want to go tomorrow? I'm off then.

Chen: I'd love to, but I can't. I'm going to the mall with my brother.

Beth: Oh, I see…what about the weekend?

Chen: I can go Saturday.

Beth: Me too!

Chen: Sounds good. Let's grab a bite before we go.

Beth: OK! Sounds perfect.

Chen: See you soon!

Listening, Part A and B

1. A: Hey, Meg. What are you doing?

   B: Oh, I just came from the mall. Look what I got.

   A: Nice! Have you played it yet?

   B: No, of course not. I just bought it. Have you played it before?

   A: No, but it looks fun.

   B: Say, do you want to come over and try it out?

   A: Now?

   B: Sure.

   A: I'd love to, but I can't. I have to go to work soon.

   B: Too bad.

   A: Let me know how you like it.

2. A: How was your class?

   B: Good. How was yours?

   A: Interesting.

   B: What are you doing now?

   A: I'm going to *Mickey's*. I'm kind of hungry.

   B: I've heard of that place. Is it any good?

   A: Yeah. Everything is cheap, and it's fast. I have another class later, so I just want a quick bite. Say, do you want to join me?

   B: Sure.

   A: But we should go now. They get pretty crowded at lunchtime.

3. A: Are you doing anything later?

   B: Not really.

   A: Do you want to see *Finders Keepers*?

   B: I'd love to! Where's it playing? At the theater?

   A: Actually, it's not playing anywhere. But I have it on DVD.

   B: Oh, it's out already?

   A: Yeah. Do you want to come over and watch it?

   B: Yeah, sure!

4. A: Hello.

   B: Jess? It's me, Parker.

   A: Hey, Parker.

   B: Listen, I'm going to *Southland* to do some shopping. Do you wanna go?

   A: *Southland?* On a Saturday afternoon?

   B: Why not? All the stores are having sales today.

   A: No, I don't think so. But thanks for asking. I need to clean my room anyway.

   B: Are you sure? It'll be fun.

   A: You can have fun for both of us.

LESSON 20

Conversation, Part A

Michelle: Hey, Lisa. Are you there yet?

Lisa: Yes. Where are you?

Michelle: I'm really sorry. I'm still on the bus. I ran an errand.

Lisa: OK. Sam isn't here yet either. How long will you be?

Michelle: Not sure. Maybe 10 minutes.

Lisa: OK. Hurry! Or we'll miss the movie.

Michelle: I'll be there soon!

Conversation, Part C

Michelle: Hey, Lisa. Are you there yet?

Lisa: Yes. Where are you?

Michelle: I'm really sorry. I'm still on the bus. I ran an errand. I had to go to the bank.

Lisa: OK. Sam isn't here yet either. How long will you be? Will you be long?

Michelle: Not sure. Maybe 10 minutes.

Lisa: OK. Hurry! Or we'll miss the movie.

Michelle: I'll be there soon!

LESSONS 17–20 ENGLISH IN ACTION

Eric: Oh, good! You're here.

Casey: Hi. I don't know where Jill is. She said she was coming.

Eric: I'm sure she'll be here shortly.

Casey: So, what do you like to do in your free time, Eric?

Eric: I like to study… and exercise!

Casey: Right. I remember… you play tennis, bowl, and box.

Eric: I am thinking of maybe starting baseball too!

Casey: Outside?

Eric: Of course.

Casey: I mean in the park, with a team.

Eric: No. But with video games, You can play anywhere. Even the park! It's almost the same thing.

Casey: I don't think it is.

Eric: Hi Maria! Have you seen Jill?

Maria: Yep! She said she was on her way down.

Eric: Hey, we're going to a movie. Do you want to join us?

Maria: I'd love to, but I can't. I have plans tonight.

Eric: Too bad. Maybe next time?

Maria: Next time. Bye.

Casey/Eric: Bye! See ya.

Eric: We're going to be late.

Casey: We have some time. We should be OK.

Jill: Sorry guys! I'm so sorry. I know, I'm late. I know. I, um, had to walk the dog.

Casey/Eric: You don't have a dog.

Jill: Right. I, um…the traffic is just awful.

Eric: What? You live right upstairs.

Jill: I know! So we should really get going or we'll be late!

LESSON 21

Conversation, Part A

Mark: So, where did you go for vacation?

Reiko: I went to Hong Kong.

Mark: Wow! Who did you go with? Did you go alone?

Reiko: No, I traveled with my sister.

Mark: How fun! And what did you do there? Did you go to Victoria Peak?

Reiko: Yeah, we also took a city tour. I took a lot of photos.

Mark: I can't wait to see them. Did you go to Hong Kong Disneyland?

Reiko: We did. It's small, but it's nice. Oh, and I went shopping.

Mark: Of course. And what did you buy me?

Conversation, Part C

Mark: So, where did you go for vacation?

Reiko: I went to Hong Kong. It was a lot of fun.

Mark: Wow! Who did you go with? Did you go alone?

Reiko: No, I traveled with my sister. It was her second time there.

Mark: How fun! And what did you do there? Did you go to Victoria Peak?

Reiko: Yeah, we also took a city tour. I took a lot of photos.

Mark: I can't wait to see them. Did you go to Hong Kong Disneyland?

Reiko: We did. It's small, but it's nice. Oh, and I went shopping.

Mark: Of course. And what did you buy me?

LESSON 22

Conversation, Part A

Annie: So Jill, I have my plane ticket to Munich. I just need to decide what to do there.

Jill: Maybe I can help, Annie. Do you prefer traveling alone or in a group?

Annie: I prefer traveling in a group. I usually have more fun with other people.

Jill: And which would you prefer—staying in hostels or staying in hotels?

Annie: I'd prefer staying in hostels. It's easier to meet people in hostels.

Jill: That's true. And would you rather travel by bus or train?

Annie: I'd rather travel by train.

Jill: OK. Then how about this six-day train tour of Bavaria? Each night you have a choice of a hotel or a hostel.

Listening, Part A and B

A: So, we need to decide on our trip. We've talked about a lot of options.

B: I agree. It's decision time.

A: OK. We've decided not to do a camping trip. And we're not interested in a spa resort vacation or a cruise. So, it's a choice between a backpacking trip and an eco-tour.

B: I'd prefer go on a backpacking trip.

A: Oh, good. Me too. I'd rather be flexible. You know—we can then do what we want.

B: I agree. We *need* to be flexible. An eco-tour would be interesting, but maybe another time.

A: So, that's good. Now how would you prefer traveling? We can go by bus or by train. The bus is cheaper and goes to more places. What do you think?

B: I'd prefer traveling by train, if that's OK.

A: I feel the same way. Trains are more interesting, I think.

B: We should look into a train pass.

A: Good idea. But let's decide where we will stay.

B: Which would you prefer—staying in hotels or hostels?

A: Definitely hostels. I want to save money.

B: So do I. Then we can spend it on other things.

A: Exactly. And what about meals?

B: There will be a lot of restaurants to choose from. But you know, I'd like to eat street food.

A: Do you think it's safe?

B: Sure. We'll just need to choose carefully.

A: Why do you prefer street food? To save money?

B: No, I just prefer trying local foods.

A: Me too.

B: So, we decided the big things. I think we'll make great travel partners.

A: I think so, too. We're both looking for the same type of trip. But there's one thing we haven't decided yet.

B: What's that?

A: Where are we going?

LESSON 23

Conversation, Part A

Teresa: Did you pack everything you need?

Miguel: Uh-huh. I just need to buy a travel pillow at the airport.

Teresa: So, this is your first overseas trip *and* your first flight! Are you nervous?

Miguel: Not at all.

Teresa: Remember, you're not allowed to take liquids on the plane.

Miguel: Really? OK. I hope I didn't forget anything.

Teresa: You must take your passport!

Miguel: Oh, of course. I guess I am a little nervous!

Conversation, Part C

Teresa: Did you pack everything you need?

Miguel: Uh-huh. I just need to buy a travel pillow at the airport.

Teresa: So, this is your first overseas trip *and* your first flight! Are you nervous?

Miguel: Not at all.

Teresa: Remember, you're not allowed to take liquids on the plane.

Miguel: Really? OK. I hope I didn't forget anything. Oh, I should get going!

Teresa: You must take your passport! You need it to get on the plane.

Miguel: Oh, of course. I guess I am a little nervous!

LESSON 24

Conversation, Part A

Tourist: Hello. How much is a one-way ticket to New York City?

Agent: It's $86.50.

Tourist: And when is the next train?

Agent: It leaves at 7:15 p.m. That's the last train of the day.

Tourist: OK. How long does it take to get there?

Agent: About three hours. It arrives at 10:20 p.m.

Tourist: And where does it depart from?

Agent: Platform four. Would you like a ticket? The train is leaving soon.

Listening, Part A and B

1. A: Next please.
   B: Hi. How much is a one-way ticket to Paris? For the next train?
   A: A single—or one-way ticket—is 58 pounds. It leaves at 4:10 p.m.
   B: OK. I'll take it. How long is the trip?
   A: Three hours.
   B: And do I leave from this station?
   A: Oh, no. You depart from Waterloo Station.
   B: Do I have enough time to get there?
   A: Oh, yes. It's only four stops away. Here's your ticket.
   B: Thank you.

2. A: Here you go.
   B: Thank you. Any bags?
   A: No, I'm just carrying this.
   B: Just a moment…oh, no. I see the flight is going to leave late.
   A: How late?
   B: Only one hour. You will leave from Gate 16.
   A: I have to transfer in Mexico City.
   B: Yes, you will still make your connection.
   A: Oh, good. Well, thank you very much.
   B: Excuse me. Don't forget your boarding pass.

3. A: Can I help you?
   B: Yes. One ticket to Ottawa, please. One-way.
   A: OK. Are you leaving today?
   B: No. It's for August 30th. I'd like to leave after 6:00 p.m.
   A: Because it's more than 21 days away, you can get a discount. The fare is $47. Canadian dollars, of course.
   B: Great.
   A: The bus leaves Toronto at 6:30 p.m. and arrives at 11:55 the same evening.
   B: That's fine. Do you know the platform?
   A: Um…no. That's a month away. I suggest you check the board that day.
   B: Of course. Thanks very much.

LESSONS 21–24 ENGLISH IN ACTION

Tom: Good day, mate!
Casey: Tom? Why are you dressed like that?

Tom: I'm crocodile Tom and this is Tommy. We're taking a trip to Tom's travels in Australia. I brought photos for you!
Casey: I didn't know you went to Australia!
Tom: I was there last year.
Casey: How long were you there? Did you travel alone?
Tom: I was there about two weeks. My cousin lives there. I have friends in Sydney, so they showed me around.
Casey: What places did you visit?
Tom: I started in Melbourne. That's where my cousin lives. We went to an amazing old market there—Queens Victoria Market. They had all sorts of stuff!
Casey: Oh, wow! That looks great. How was the weather there? Was it cold?
Tom: Yeah, it was a little cool there, so you need to take a jacket. Then I went to Sydney. Look here. You have to take a boat trip to the harbor.
Casey: That looks nice.
Tom: After that I went to the Gold Coast. That's north of Sydney. There are beautiful beaches there.
Casey: Wow. It almost looks like real gold. Did you get around by bus?
Tom: No. Actually, I prefer traveling by plane. Australia is a huge country so bus trips take too long. By bus, it takes about…eight hours to get to Sydney from Melbourne.
Casey: Oh yeah. That's long. So what else did you do?
Tom: I went up the coast and went scuba diving in the Great Barrier Reef. You must go there!
Casey: Absolutely!
Tom: Oh, and this was the best part of the trip. I went to the most amazing park—Kakadu National Park.
Casey: That's gorgeous.
Tom: You can camp there, go hiking, and even make new friends! Casey? Can do me a favor while you're in Australia?
Casey: Yeah. Sure. What is it?
Tom: Well, I made a cool friend at Kakadu National Park. Will you say hi?

Casey: Sure. How will I find your friend? Do you have an e-mail address?

Tom: No, but he lives at the park. Take this.

Casey: Tom!

Tom: What?

Casey: That's a crocodile!

Tom: His name's Tommy. I named this after him. Please say hi!

LESSON 25

Conversation, Part A

Susan: The music is great, and I love your clothes. Are they traditional?

Calum: Oh, yes. You probably know this—it's called a kilt.

Susan: Yeah. I've seen them in pictures. Is it a kind of skirt?

Calum: Well, Scottish men don't really call it a *skirt*. People usually wear it on special occasions.

Susan: I see. I love the pattern.

Calum: The pattern is plaid. Scotland is famous for them. The pattern can tell you what family someone is from.

Susan: How interesting! Is there a traditional outfit for women as well?

Calum: Yes. Women normally wear longer skirts. But when they dance, they may wear kilts. I think there will be a women's dance performance later.

Conversation, Part C

Susan: The music is great, and I love your clothes. Are they traditional?

Calum: Oh, yes. You probably know this—it's called a kilt. Have you heard of it?

Susan: Yeah. I've seen them in pictures. Is it a kind of skirt?

Calum: Well, Scottish men don't really call it a *skirt*. People usually wear it on special occasions. They don't wear it every day.

Susan: I see. I love the pattern.

Calum: The pattern is plaid. Scotland is famous for them. The pattern can tell you what family someone is from.

Susan: How interesting! Is there a traditional outfit for women as well?

Calum: Yes. Women normally wear longer skirts. But when they dance, they may wear kilts. I think there will be a women's dance performance later.

LESSON 26

Conversation

Tom: Ana, I really want a new jacket. What do you think? Is it me?

Ana: Not really, Tom. I would get something more practical. And the quality is poor.

Tom: Yeah, you're right. Do you think this design is nice?

Ana: Um…a different design might be better.

Tom: How about this one?

Ana: Honestly, you might want to try a different color. That one doesn't really suit you.

Tom: Really?

Ana: This one will look better on you.

Tom: I have that exact jacket at home. You're picky, but you have good taste!

Listening, Part A and B

1. A: I just can't find anything I like today.
   B: Let's keep looking. I'm sure we can find something.
   A: Hey, look at these. These are nice. Oh, and look—a brand name. You know how I like brand name clothes.
   B: Do I ever! Are they long enough?
   A: Yeah. So, what do you think?
   B: Well, the quality looks good, but I would get a different color.
   A: Really?
   B: Yeah, I'm not sure it's your best color. It will be hard to match shoes to that color.

2. A: Hey, come over here.
   B: Yeah?
   A: Look at this. Isn't it cool?
   B: Yeah. The dark color looks great on you. Does it fit?
   A: Perfectly. It's warm, too.
   B: I love the design.
   A: I do, too. And it's so soft. Feel it.

B: How much is it?

A: It's um…oh, my.

B: Wow! That's a lot of money.

A: I know. I could charge it.

B: You know, a cheaper one might be better. Let's keep looking.

3. A: I really want something to go with my new pants. Please help.

B: OK, just relax.

A: What about this?

B: It's nice. I like the design a lot. And the colors, too. But…

A: But what?

B: It looks cheap. The material looks cheap.

A: You think so?

B: Yeah. I think that's why it's not so expensive. You might want to look at brand names.

A: Brand names? But they're too expensive.

B: Not always. Let's see if there's anything on sale.

4. A: Come over here. There are some great deals.

B: Hm…do you see anything you like?

A: How about these? They're 40% off. What a bargain.

B: But do you like them?

A: Well, I like the price.

B: Maybe, you could find a different design.

A: Yeah, you're right. A different design would be better.

B: They're a good value for the money, but will you wear them?

A: Maybe not. They would probably just sit on the floor of my closet. Hey! Look here. These are 50% off!

LESSON 27

Conversation, Part A

Jake: Hello.

Ben: Hi, Jake. It's me, Ben. Are you still at the home decor store?

Jake: Yeah, I just found the lamp we looked at online. It will look great in our new apartment.

Ben: Oh, good. Listen, can you do me a favor?

Jake: Sure.

Ben: Would you get some pillows for the sofa?

Jake: No problem. Do you want any particular color?

Ben: How about green?

Jake: Sure. Anything else?

Ben: Would you mind picking up a mirror, too?

Jake: Not at all. Do we need anything else?

Ben: Actually…can you pick up some food? Our fridge is empty.

Conversation, Part C

Jake: Hello.

Ben: Hi, Jake. It's me, Ben. Are you still at the home decor store?

Jake: Yeah, I just found the lamp we looked at online. It will look great in our new apartment. And it's on sale.

Ben: Oh, good. Listen, can you do me a favor?

Jake: Sure. What do you need?

Ben: Would you get some pillows for the sofa?

Jake: No problem. Do you want any particular color?

Ben: How about green

Jake: Sure. Anything else?

Ben: Would you mind picking up a mirror, too?

Jake: Not at all. Do we need anything else?

Ben: Actually…can you pick up some food? Our fridge is empty.

LESSON 28

Conversation

Dave: Hi, Helena. Are you busy?

Helena: Not really. What you are doing?

Dave: I'm playing with my new tablet. I just got it.

Helena: I need to get one of those. They're so cool looking. What do you use it for?

Dave: Lots of things. I mostly use it to store photos and watch movies. It's so much better than my phone.

Helena: What is its most interesting feature?

Dave: The most useful feature is probably the editing software. I can use it for recording, editing, and sharing my own music.

Helena: How fun!

Listening, Part B

1. This the perfect item for the musician "wannabe" in all of us. Some of us play a musical instrument, but it's not always practical to carry it around with us. Well, that problem is now solved with the Electric Guitar Bag. This unique bag combines a normal bag with an actual guitar. You can use it to carry a laptop, or use it to relax and relieve stress. If you're feeling stressed, just rock out and you'll feel better in no time! Order now for just $49.99.

2. Do you like Asian food, but find you aren't so good with chopsticks? Do you get embarrassed when you have to ask for a fork in a Chinese or Japanese restaurant? Well, let these five pandas in the Panda Chopsticks Kit help you. They are small, plastic, and slippery, so you get lots of practice trying to pick them up with your chopsticks. Use the chopsticks to place them in different positions. Just remember not to eat the pandas. Each set costs $24.

3. Five plus five equals 20, right? If you said wrong, you are right. With the Wrongulator calculator five plus five might equal 20, 12, or 200—anything, *but* the correct answer of ten. Whatever you put into the Wrongulator is guaranteed to produce a wrong answer. You can't use it to get a correct answer, so what would you use this for? Most people just use it to play tricks on people—to have a laugh. They may give it as a gift to someone in their office. The cost? Only $7.

4. Here's something for the person who has everything—a Clone Doll. Get a perfect likeness of yourself. The company that makes these dolls takes a photo of you in 3D and produces a doll head of you. The process is not difficult thanks to 3D scanners and printers. The doll head is then attached to a variety of doll bodies. Now, what in the world are these used for? The most popular use is for weddings. But it seems some people like to use the dolls to scare others! Each doll costs $1,800.

LESSONS 25–28 ENGLISH IN ACTION

Jill: That's all you're packing?

Casey: Yes. I prefer to pack light.

Jill: OK. What do people usually wear in Australia?

Tom: It depends. Students generally wear T-shirts and jeans, if it's warm.

Casey: In that case, I think I have all the clothes I'll need.

Jill: It might get cold there.

Casey: But it will be summer.

Jill: Still. You never know. I have a thick sweater. You can borrow mine.

Casey: OK. Thanks, Jill.

Tom: Do you have boots for hiking?

Casey: I don't know if I'll go hiking. But I do have boots!

Casey: What do think? Isn't the design nice?

Tom: I would get something more practical.

Jill: I have great hiking boots.

Casey: Would you mind if I borrowed them?

Jill: Not at all! Let me get everything.

Casey: I don't know if I'll have room.

Eric: Hi guys! What are you doing?

Tom: We're helping Casey pack.

Eric: Sounds like fun! Do you have a book to read for the plane?

Casey: No…but I have my tablet. I use it to play games, watch movies, read books…Just about everything!

Eric: What if the battery runs out?

Casey: Well…

Eric: See? Then you won't have anything to do. Don't worry! I have lots of books you can borrow.

Casey: OK…

Eric: I'll go get them.

Tom: OK. And I have some things you will definitely need including—a first-aid kit.

Casey: Right…

Jill: Here Casey!

Casey: Oh! It will be warm there. I don't think I need all of this.

Jill: Of course you do!

Casey: OK, thanks Jill.

Eric: Hey Casey! You're going to love these books! And I found something else you might need!

Casey: Huh?

Eric: These books are great! And you'll need the snorkel and flippers when you go in the water.

Casey: Geez. Thanks Eric.

Eric: No problem!

Tom: Hey Casey. Lucky you! I found everything!

Casey: Oh! Oh, boy.

LESSON 29

Conversation, Part A

Angela: Let's pause the movie and get a snack. Isn't the movie exciting, Sonya?

Sonya: Not really. I think it's boring. I feel like the acting isn't very good.

Angela: Really?

Sonya: Yeah, and to me, the story is kind of confusing.

Angela: I like it actually. In my opinion, the story is excellent.

Sonya: If you ask me, the story could be better.

Angela: Then why don't we watch something else? I can finish this movie later.

Sonya: No, no, that's fine. I do want to see how it ends.

Listening, Part A and B

1. Maria: Hey, Jason? Have you read this?

   Jason: Let's see…oh, *The Case of the Missing Briefcase*. Yeah.

   Maria: What did you think of it?

   Jason: It's one of my favorite books. A real page-turner.

   Maria: Are you serious?

   Jason: Yeah. I found the story very interesting. I take it you didn't like it?

   Maria: Not at all. I thought it was really, really boring.

   Jason: Huh. I guess you won't go see the movie next year then.

   Maria: No way.

2. Jason: Can you help me?

   Maria: With what?

   Jason: Today's homework. I'm finding the assignment confusing.

   Maria: Really? I've already finished it.

Jason: You have? You weren't confused?

Maria: No. I thought it was difficult but not confusing.

Jason: Well maybe you can explain it to me.

Maria: Of course. So, what part exactly?

3. Jason: Can you hand me the remote control?

   Maria: Why? I thought you liked soccer.

   Jason: I love soccer, but I don't think this match is very exciting. Nothing is happening.

   Maria: But someone will probably score after you change the channel.

   Jason: What do you think of this match?

   Maria: It's not exciting, but there isn't anything else on. Why don't we watch a little more?

   Jason: OK. But I'm getting a snack.

LESSON 30

Conversation, Part A

Zack: Hi Caitlin. It's Zack. Listen, I don't mean to gossip, but did you hear that Joey and Mike got into an argument?

Caitlin: I just heard. Our two best friends…

Zack: I don't really know what happened. To me, they just stopped communicating.

Caitlin: I think so, too. But I feel it's probably more than that. I think Mike sometimes argued with Joey and that bothered him.

Zack: I'm not sure I really agree. I've seen Joey judging Mike.

Caitlin: I just hope they make up or at least stay friends.

Zack: I feel the same way. Let's be sure to be there for them.

Conversation, Part C

Zack: Hi, Caitlin. It's Zack. Listen, I don't mean to gossip, but did you hear that Joey and Mike got into an argument?

Caitlin: I just heard. Our two best friends…I feel so bad for them.

Zack: I don't really know what happened. To me, they just stopped communicating.

Caitlin: I think so, too. But I feel it's probably more than that. I think Mike sometimes argued with Joey and that bothered him.

Zack: I'm not sure I really agree. I've seen Joey judging Mike. That wasn't nice.

Caitlin: I just hope they make up or at least stay friends.

Zack: I feel the same way. Let's be sure to be there for them.

LESSON 31

Conversation, Part A

Kevin: I am so embarrassed.

Amy: Why? What happened?

Kevin: I thought Sandra's birthday was on Sunday night. But it was on Saturday night.

Amy: Oh, no. So, you missed it?

Kevin: What do you think I should do?

Amy: I'd just be honest. And definitely apologize. I'd make sure to get her a birthday present, too!

Kevin: What time does the mall close?

Listening, Part A and B

1. I got home a little late last night. It was actually my birthday, but I was too busy at work to plan anything. My friend borrowed my apartment key yesterday morning. He said he'd left something there a few days ago, and wanted to pick it up. Anyway, when I got home the place was totally dark. When I turned on the light, a whole bunch of my friends were there and they all shouted, "Surprise! Happy birthday!"

2. Some new people moved into the apartment next door to me a few weeks ago. I haven't met them yet, and I never see them anywhere around the apartment building. But late at night I hear some strange noises coming from their apartment. It sounds like they're making something. Sometimes, I hear a sound as if someone is playing a strange musical instrument. What would you do if you were me?

3. I borrowed a book from a friend a few weeks ago. It was a book her mother gave her, and I know she really liked it. Unfortunately, I spilled some coffee on it. I tried to clean it up,

but now several pages have awful coffee stains on them. She won't be happy with me at all. What should I do?

4. I ran into an old friend of mine at the train station the other day. The last time I saw her was two years ago. She looked great, and we're going to get together again for coffee this week. The only thing was that when I first ran into her, I couldn't remember her name. Has that ever happened to you? Luckily, I don't think she noticed.

LESSON 32

Conversation, Part A

Walt: I heard something interesting on the news last night before I went to bed.

Tara: Oh, yeah? What's that?

Walt: It was a story about a woman who gave away several million dollars. It was money she inherited from an aunt.

Tara: Wow! What did she do with it?

Walt: She was watching a TV show about needy families. After watching the show, she decided to give all the money away.

Tara: Amazing.

Walt: Next, she set up a scholarship program to pay for the education of hundreds of motivated high school kids. Then she decided to pay for their college tuition, too.

Tara: That's fantastic. She must be *really* generous!

Conversation, Part C

Walt: I heard something interesting on the news last night before I went to bed.

Tara: Oh, yeah? What's that?

Walt: It was a story about a woman who gave away several million dollars. It was money she inherited from an aunt.

Tara: Wow! What did she do with it?

Walt: She was watching a TV show about needy families. After watching the show, she decided to give all the money away. Can you believe that?

Tara: Amazing.

Walt: Next, she set up a scholarship program to pay for the education of hundreds of motivated high school kids. Then she decided to pay for their college tuition, too. What a generous person!

Tara: That's fantastic. She must be really generous.

LESSONS 29–32 ENGLISH IN ACTION

Casey: Hello? Hello? Can you hear me?

Jill/Maria/Tom: Hi Casey!!

Casey: Hi everyone!

Jill: How do you like Sydney?

Casey: I love it! I think it's an amazing city. Everyone is really nice and the city is just beautiful.

Tom: Did you go to Kakadu National Park yet?

Casey: Not yet. I just got here.

Maria: How's the weather?

Casey: It's warm during the day and colder at night. But I have lots of sweaters, thanks to Jill.

Jill: Yay!

Casey: I have to tell you guys something that happened.

Maria: What happened?

Eric: Tell us!

Tom: What?

Jill: Sure!

Casey: Before I got to my hotel, I was really excited. But when I got to my hotel, I felt awful! It was nothing like the pictures.

Jill: Oh no!

Casey: I complained, but they wouldn't give me my money back.

Maria: That's terrible.

Casey: After that I left to find another hotel. I was walking around when I noticed something.

Tom: What? What?

Casey: I found a wallet. There was a lot of money in it, but no ID.

Eric: How much was it?

Casey: Around 3,000 U.S. dollars. What would you do if you found all that money?

Tom: Wow.

Jill: That's a lot of money.

Maria: If I were you, I'd give it to the police.

Tom: I'm not sure I agree. You could stay at a nicer hotel!

Jill: I don't know what I would do.

Eric: I would be honest and give it to the police.

Maria: I feel exactly the same way.

Casey: OK. So, guess what I did?

Jill: You kept it!

Tom: You spent it!

Casey: Nope. I did what Eric and Maria would do and gave it to the police. And guess that?

Jill/Tom/Eric/Maria: What?

Casey: As soon as I turned it in, the man who lost the wallet contacted me! It turns out that he owns one of the best hotels in Sydney!

Tom: No way!

Casey: Yes way! So I get to stay for free!

Eric: That's awesome!

Tom: Wow!

Maria: See, it pays to be honest.

Casey: I have to go, I have a tour, but I'll see you guys again soon!

Eric/Tom: Bye Casey!

Maria: Travel safe!

Jill: Be careful!

Tom: Can I see Tommy?

Casey: Bye guys!

Eric/Tom/Maria/Jill: Bye!

Vocabulary Index

LESSON 10

climb stairs
dance to music
do chores
follow a workout video
jump up and down
play an active video game
rearrange the furniture
ride a bike
walk around the neighborhood

LESSON 11

activity
ballroom dancing
bowling
calories burned
ice skating
racquetball
running
skiing
swimming
tae kwon do
tai chi
walking

LESSON 12

baseball
basketball
bowling
boxing
cycling
fishing
hockey
indoor sports
outdoor sports
tennis
volleyball

LESSON 13

arts
biologist
education
fashion designer
graphic designer
health

journalist
nurse
professor
psychologist
science
surgeon

LESSON 14

cashier
chef
doctor
fire fighter
flight attendant
pilot
police officer
pop singer
server

LESSON 15

blogger
doesn't need a car
film director
flight attendant
gets long vacations
homemaker
makes good money
stands all day
travels for free
works on weekends

LESSON 16

a company's reputation
benefits
colleagues
hours
location
responsibilities
salary
size of the company

LESSON 17

chat online
listen to music
play sports
play video games

read
shop
sleep in
watch TV

LESSON 18

action
animated
comedy
historical drama
horror
romantic comedy
science fiction
thriller

LESSON 19

beach
bookstore
coffee shop
library
mall
movie theater
museum
park
pool
theme park

LESSON 20

broke down
couldn't find
lost track
needed to
ran into
stuck in

LESSON 21

go shopping
go to museums
go to the theatre
see historical sights
see sporting events
take photos
take tours
try local food
visit markets

VOCABULARY INDEX

OXFORD
UNIVERSITY PRESS

198 Madison Avenue
New York, NY 10016 USA

Great Clarendon Street, Oxford, OX2 6DP, United Kingdom

Oxford University Press is a department of the University of Oxford.
It furthers the University's objective of excellence in research, scholarship,
and education by publishing worldwide. Oxford is a registered trade
mark of Oxford University Press in the UK and in certain other countries.

General Manager, American ELT: Laura Pearson
Executive Publishing Manager: Erik Gundersen
Managing Editor: Jennifer Meldrum
Associate Editor: Hana Yoo
Director, ADP: Susan Sanguily
Executive Design Manager: Maj-Britt Hagsted
Associate Design Manager: Michael Steinhofer
Image Manager: Trisha Masterson
Art Editor: Joe Kassner
Electronic Production Manager: Julie Armstrong
Production Artist: Elissa Santos
Production Coordinator: Brad Tucker

ISBN: 978 0 19 403016 8 Student Book 2 (pack)
ISBN: 978 0 19 403001 4 Student Book 2 (pack component)
ISBN: 978 0 19 403022 9 Access Card 2 (pack component)
ISBN: 978 0 19 403025 0 Online Practice 2 (pack component)

Printed in China
This book is printed on paper from certified and well-managed sources.

ACKNOWLEDGEMENTS

Illustrations by: Barb Bastian: 19, 57, 59; Kenneth Batelman: 66; Bunky Hurter:
6, 22(b), 42, 64; Neil Jeffrey: 5, 14, 23, 56; Javier Joaquin: 4, 22(t), 32, 76; Tracey
Knight: 24, 34; Tony Randazzo: 69; Gavin Reece: 18, 36, 54, 72; Heidi Schmidt:
15, 65; Simon Shaw: 67.

Commissioned photography by: Richard Hutchings/Digital Light Source, Cover
photo of person speaking and cast shot on page ii; People's Television, Inc., all
video stills.

*The publishers would like to thank the following for their kind permission to reproduce
photographs*: Cover (waterfall) Micha Pawlitzki/Corbis, (ice climber) Brand
X Pictures/Oxford University Press, (dancer) Russell Illig/Getty images,
(background montage) PhotoAlto/Sigrid Olsson/Getty images, Howard
Kingsnorth/Cultura/Getty images, Christopher Futcher/istockphoto.
com, Fabrice LEROUGE/Getty images, PhotoAlto/Getty images, Andresr/
shutterstock.com, Monkey Business Images/shutterstock.com, Ferran Traite
Soler/istockphoto.com, PhotoAlto/Sigrid Olsson/Getty images; pg. 2 ONOKY
- Photononstop /Alamy; pg. 3 C. Devan/Corbis; pg. 5 GYI NSEA/istockphoto.
com; pg. 7 White Packert /The Image Bank/Getty Images; pg. 8 Lane Oatey/Blue
Jean Images/Getty Images; pg. 9 Alexander Chaikin/shutterstock.com; pg. 12
Niko Guido/istockphoto.com; pg. 13 (a) Oxford University Press, (b) Mosquito.
name/shutterstock.com, © Edward Westmacott/shutterstock.com, (d) matin/
shutterstock.com; pg. 14 (grill) Mike Lang/Flickr/Getty Images, (bake) Rudi
Gobbo/istockphoto.com, (fry)PeJo/shutterstock.com, (steam) Foodcollection
RF/Getty Images, (boil) fredredhat/shutterstock.com, (microwave) Don
Nichols/istockphoto.com; pg. 16 (sarah) Supri Suharjoto/shutterstock.com,
(Kit) Jason Stitt/shutterstock.com, (restaurant) ivylingpy/shutterstock.com;
pg. 17 slava296/shutterstock.com; pg. 23 Paul Harizan/StockImage/Getty
Images; pg. 25 Food Centrale Hamburg GmbH /Alamy; pg. 26 Tim Platt/
Iconica/Getty Images; pg. 27 (archery) David De Lossy/Photodisc/Getty Images,
(kayaking) technotr/istockphoto.com, (table tennis) Amwell/Stone/Getty
Images, (water aerobics) Georgiy Pashin/istockphoto.com, (zumba) Richard
Levine /Alamy, (forza) Thinkstock/Comstock Images/Getty Images, (Bosu
ball) Stephen VanHorn /Alamy; pg. 28 (Celine) Juanmonino/istockphoto.com,
(Doug) Valua Vitaly/istockphoto.com, (tennis match) Bob Thomas/Stone/Getty
Images; pg. 29 Warren Jacobi/Corbis; pg. 33 Terry Vine/Stone/Getty Images;
pg. 34 Walter Lockwood/Workbook Stock/Getty Images; pg. 35 Dave Bartruff/
CORBIS; pg. 37 (zookeeper) Joel Sartore/National Geographic/Getty Images,
(ballet dancer) Kaziyeva-Dem'yanenko Svitlana/shutterstock.com, (plumber)
Kurhan/shutterstock.com, (candy store owner) White Packert/The Image
Bank/Getty Images; pg. 38 (manager) Jack Hollingsworth/Photodisc/Getty
Images, (Evan) Valua Vitaly/istockphoto.com, (tour guide) Getty Images/Getty
Images; pg. 39 News/Getty Images; pg. 40(tl) Jorn Georg Tomter/Digital Vision/
Getty Images; pg. 43 Marcel Jancovic/shutterstock.com; pg. 44 (Jeff) Joshua
Hodge Photography/istockphoto.com, (Kirk) Luis Santos/shutterstock.com,
(rock climbing) John & Eliza Forder/Stone/Getty Images; pg. 45 Stephan Zabel/
istockphoto.com; pg. 46 (Beth) Oxford University Press, (Chen) Fancy/Oxford
University Press; pg. 47 (beach) Pierre-Yves Babelon/shutterstock.com, (pencil)
Dennis Kitchen Studio, Inc/Oxford University Press; pg. 48 Chris Gramly/
istockphoto.com; 48 (b) jonya/istockphoto.com; pg. 49 Steve Lovegrove/
shutterstock.com; pg. 52 Naki Kouyioumtzis/Axiom Photographic Agency/
Getty Images; pg. 53 Alan Bailey/Getty Images; pg. 55 Maugli/shutterstock.
com; pg. 58 (subway) ack/istockphoto.com, (tourist) Alen/shutterstock.com,
(agent) Fuse/Getty Images, (NYC skyline) Songquan Deng/shutterstock.com;
pg. 60 (b) Gordon Bell/shutterstock.com, © Ian Scott/shutterstock.com, (d)
Sebastien Burel/shutterstock.com; pg. 62 (Susan) Fotosearch/Oxford University
Press, (Calum) Bill Bachmann /Alamy; pg. 63 Rachel Watson/Stone/Getty
Images; pg. 65 Nick Dolding/Stone/Getty Images; pg. 66 (Jake) Comstock
Images/Getty Images, (Ben) Lane Oatey/Getty Images; pg. 68 Corbis; pg. 69
Hype Photography/Stone/Getty Images; pg. 73 Chris Whitehead/Cultura/Getty
Images; pg. 74 (Zack) ML Harris/Iconica/Getty Images, (Caitlin) Nicolas Russell/
Photodisc/Getty Images; pg. 75 Lynch, Mark/Cartoon Stock; pg. 77 smoxx/
shutterstock.com; pg. 78 STOCK4B Creative/Getty Images; pg. 79 Samuel
Lara Hernández/Flickr/Getty Images; pg. 80 (b) Jeff Spielman/Photographer's
Choice/Getty Images; pgs. 82 & 90 (a) Elena Elisseeva/shutterstock.com,
(b) Valua Vitaly/shutterstock.com, © Supri Suharjoto/shutterstock.com,
(d) Dedyukhin Dmitry/shutterstock.com, (e) ostill/shutterstock.com, (f)
Andresr/shutterstock.com, (g) Warren Goldswain/shutterstock.com, (h) Felix
Mizioznikov/shutterstock.com, (i) Warren Goldswain/shutterstock.com, (j)
Anton Albert/shutterstock.com, (k) wong yu liang/shutterstock.com, (l) Felix
Mizioznikov/shutterstock.com, (m) Jason Stitt/shutterstock.com, (n) Jason
Stitt/shutterstock.com, (o) leungchopan/shutterstock.com, (p) Valua Vitaly/
shutterstock.com, (q) Blend Images/shutterstock.com, (r) szefei/shutterstock.
com, (s) Felix Mizioznikov/shutterstock.com, (t) AISPIX by Image Source/
shutterstock.com; pgs. 88 & 96 (swiss army knife) Shane White/shutterstock.
com, (SUV) Rob Wilson/shutterstock.com, (chair) Adam Fraise/shutterstock.
com, (screwdriver) Oleg Golovnev/shutterstock.com, (trash can) Lusoimages/
shutterstock.com, (stroller) fonats/shutterstock.com, (baby sling) Kozlovskaya
Ksenia/shutterstock.com, (duct tape) Feng Yu/shutterstock.com, (string)
Sharon Day/shutterstock.com, (scissors) Zvyagintsev Sergey/shutterstock.com,
(swing) tkemot/shutterstock.com, (measuring cup) Mark Herreid/shutterstock.
com, (backpack) kedrov/shutterstock.com, (shelf) barbaliss/shutterstock.com,
(tote bag) Cathleen A Clapper/shutterstock.com.

Additional photography provided by: Asia Images Group Pte Ltd/Alamy, Aldo
Murillo/istockphoto.com, Neustockimages/istockphoto.com (speaking images
in top border); DPiX Center/shutterstock.com (brushed metal texture in side
border).

Video: People's Television, Inc /www.ppls.tv